BOOKS BY MARIE COLE POWELL

GUIDING THE EXPERIENCE OF
WORSHIP

JUNIOR METHOD IN THE
CHURCH SCHOOL

GUIDING THE EXPERIENCE OF WORSHIP

MARIE COLE POWELL

Printed for

The
Leadership Training Publishing Association

By
Abingdon - Cokesbury Press
New York   Nashville

Copyright, MCMXXXV, by
MARIE COLE POWELL

Printed in the United States of America

CONTENTS

CHAPTER   PAGE

       EDITOR'S INTRODUCTION 5

       AUTHOR'S INTRODUCTION 7

  I. WHAT IS WORSHIP? 11

 II. AIDS TO WORSHIP 30

III. MAKING GOD REAL 54

 IV. PLANNING THE WORSHIP PROGRAM OF THE
        CHURCH 85

  V. THE SERVICE OF WORSHIP . . . 107

 VI. MATERIALS OF WORSHIP 122

VII. VISUALIZATION MATERIALS IN WORSHIP . 147

VIII. MUSIC IN WORSHIP 171

 IX. PRAYER IN WORSHIP 202

  X. PREPARATION FOR WORSHIP . . . 225

 XI. THE LEADERSHIP OF WORSHIP . . . 244

     APPENDIX A 261

     APPENDIX B (CHART) 263

EDITOR'S INTRODUCTION

"THE curriculum is ninety per cent teacher." This assertion is being made by Christian educators with more and more conviction. If the statement is essentially true, the development of a consecrated and skilled staff of leaders is the first responsibility of a teaching church. The past decade has witnessed a rapid improvement in curriculum materials, and many have expected that, in some mysterious way, teaching methods would advance automatically. But, too often, these better materials in the hands of untrained leaders have produced disappointment and discouragement. The training of leaders for the teaching task must parallel the introduction of higher types of curricula.

Denominational education boards are therefore laying greater stress than formerly upon the training of a leadership qualified for the educational work of the local church. Their efforts, through both denominational and interdenominational channels, have not been without reward. The past dozen years have seen a remarkable growth in the number of leaders in training. The chief problem confronting the friends of leadership training to-day is that of how to develop actual skill in teaching rather than a mere verbal acquaintance with a few psychological laws.

In making available for the leadership-training program materials which are educationally sound and relatively inexpensive, the Leadership Training Publishing Association is rendering a unique service. This Association is an unincorporated group of representatives of the educational, editorial, and publishing agencies of "such evangelical denominations as may desire to co-operate in the purposes of the Association," which are "to prepare and publish through the denominational houses, materials needed in the conduct of the leadership-training program of the co-operating denominations." Through its various committees the Association selects writers, circulates outlines and manuscripts for rigid criticism, and publishes those which meet the high requirements of the present-day training program.

Guiding the Experience of Worship deals with a subject which is receiving increasing recognition as an indispensable element in our total program of religious education. It is written from the point of view of the church school as a whole and gives both an understanding of the nature of this high experience and a large amount of practical help in its stimulation and guidance.

The author, Mrs. Marie Cole Powell, has long been identified with progressive movements in the field of religious education. She has had a successful experience as a director and as an instructor in training schools. At the present time she is a member of the faculty of Boston University School of Religious Education and Social Service. From the standpoint of both theory and practical experience in the field of her subject we believe no better writer could have been selected for this book.

The use of this volume both as a text in training classes and for individual reading and study should have fruitful outcomes in the improvement of the worship activities of our church schools. The Association heartily commends it to its constituency.

ERWIN L. SHAVER, *Chairman,*
Editorial and Educational Committee.

AUTHOR'S INTRODUCTION

WITH all the changing conceptions of the function of the Christian Church and the questions that are sometimes raised about its ultimate destiny, one conviction seems to be increasingly gaining in strength, namely, that worship is the chief concern of the church, and should be the very center of its ministry. Whether we note the eagerness with which many turn from the bewilderment of modern life to seek assurance in communion with God or whether we regret the large number of empty pews on Sunday mornings, either the failure or the success of the church in touching the lives of people to-day indicates the need for a revival of worship which will minister to the spiritual aspirations of the modern world.

We are living in a day when men and women are seeking for reality in their religious experience. Many long to be assured that they may seek and find God, that they may knock and that in response a door will be opened for them into a world of spiritual values which cannot be shaken. Through the ministry of worship the church may guide men in their quest for God, and open the door which leads into life eternal.

In this book worship is considered as a vital experience through which children, young people, and adults may find a deeper meaning in all other experiences. Worship is thought of as that conscious relationship with God which glorifies the commonplace, provides courage with which to face life, helps the individual to grow in character, and furnishes the incentive to remove social injustices, and to build the kingdom of God on this earth.

It is an almost impossible task to write a book on worship which shall embody all the traditions as well as all the hopes of widely different groups. Partly because worship is so intensely personal an experience, we each approach it with different interests. Because there have grown up distinct traditions of worship in different communions, each individual is conditioned by his religious culture in some tradition. In a brief text, it is practically inevitable that some points of view may seem slighted and that others shall appear unduly emphasized. No one is more conscious of these possibilities than is the author. But it is hoped that the treatment of worship is catholic enough to enable readers to find a place for their own interpretations, and at the same time keep an open mind for other approaches.

It is hoped that through the study of this book church groups and others may find some inspiration for their task of planning the worship program of the church, that they may find practical suggestions for carrying out that program, and that they may feel an incentive to explore further to discover what the experience of worship may mean in the lives of men and women, young people, and little children to-day. If, as they thus think and plan, there should come to them the deepening of their own fellowship with God, they may say, with all reverence with Jesus, "I and my Father are one," and dedicate themselves anew to this high calling of God— the leadership of worship.

The author wishes to express her appreciation to the many who, in training schools, have read this book in manuscript form and have given valuable and constructive suggestions, to the members of the Leadership Training Publishing Association who have rendered helpful and enlightening criticism, and to the publishers who have granted permission to quote from their sources.

Every effort has been made to trace the ownership of all copyrighted material. Should any infringement have unconsciously been made, the author fully desires to express her regrets, and will be glad to make proper acknowledgment in future editions of the book.

MARIE COLE POWELL.

CHAPTER I

WHAT IS WORSHIP?

Where the sun shines in the street
There are very many feet
Seeking God, all unaware
That their seeking is a prayer.
I wonder would they deem it odd
  (Who think they are on business bent)
  If some one went
And told them, "You are seeking God."

MARY CAROLYN DAVIES,

—From "Feet," found in *World's Great Religious
Poetry,* edited by Caroline M. Hill, p. 34.

AT the heart of worship lies a fundamental human
need—the need of God. At the heart of living lies this
same fundamental need—the need for courage to face
the facts of life, for inner peace and harmony to enable
us to live life confidently; the need for vitality to live
the creative life; the need for a companionship of the
spirit that we may not live alone. By whatever name
we call it, it indicates a need of God.

In an age when competition is keen, when life is full
to overflowing with activity, when the din and roar of
a machine-made world deafen our spirits to the call of
the spiritual, when the rush and intensity of life tend
to crowd out or push into the fringe of consciousness
our interest in that more abundant life—in such an age
the need of God is insistent. We are living in a generation when the power of *things* is tremendous. In our
eager grasp for the things of this life, so much more
within the reach of all of us than formerly, we may lose
sight of those "things which are eternal."

11

GUIDING THE EXPERIENCE OF WORSHIP

This need of God is universal. We read it in the faces of over-anxious, dissatisfied men and women, in the listless, unhappy faces of others, in the feverish external activity with which we seek to forget our unsatisfied cravings for peace. We note it in the impetus with which people to-day are driven toward any cult which seems to offer happiness and freedom from pain and anxiety. We note it "where cross the crowded ways of life." And who will say that the boys and girls that are living the formative years of their lives in the midst of this changing civilization do not need to feel, more than all others, that "underneath are the everlasting arms"?

Outside the church near Toynbee Hall, in London, there used to hang this invitation:

Your lives are busy, useful, honest; but your faces are anxious and you are not all you want to be. There is within you another life, a buried life, which does not get free. When it really hears God's voice, it will arise. I don't think this life will be stirred by excitement. I believe that in the quiet of a place full of good memories, in the sound of fine music, in the sympathy of fellow seekers, we may better wait God's call. It may be that as you listen to the silence, to the music, or to the worship of others, God will speak, that the buried life will arise, and that you will have peace.

Each individual brings to his experience of God the same background and point of view which he brings to any other of life's great experiences. Whatever the causes of these individual differences, the need for God remains the same, even though the reason for that need and the form in which it is expressed may vary.

"The way I go—no other feet have trod.
And no one walks the road with me but God."[1]

[1] "Life-Death," by Grace Noll Crowell, *Century Magazine*, March, 1928. D. Appleton-Century Company. Used by permission of publishers and author.

WHAT IS WORSHIP?

Since we feel this need for God in the midst of life, and since in worship this need struggles to express itself and finds God there to meet the need, the problem is how to bring worship into life. How shall these many seekers after God become aware of him? How may worship help them to do so?

We should remind ourselves too that the many seekers after God are not all adults. In childhood the great search begins. "What does God look like?" inquires the four-year-old at the bedtime hour. "Is he here in the dark?" "Why can't we see him?" "How do we know he is here?"

Professor Will Durant tells the story of his little girl who came to her mother one day with the age-old question, "Mother, what is God like?" The mother hesitated in the presence of so great a question and finally said, "Dear, ask your daddy." So the little girl went to her father with her search after God. "Daddy, what is God like?" And he too hesitated. Later on, among her childish possessions they found a slip of paper with a bit of free verse inscribed on it. It went something like this:

"I asked my mother what God was like,
  She did not know.
  I asked my teacher what God was like,
  She did not know.
  Then I asked my father, who knows more than anyone
  Else in the whole world, what God was like.
  He did not know.
  I think if I had lived as long as
  My mother, or my father,
  I would know something about God."

We hear a great deal to-day about the rights of the child, his right to be well-born, his right to play, his right to an education, his right to conditions of physical

13

and mental hygiene. Surely, along with all these other rights there stands his right to an awareness of God.

WHAT WORSHIP IS

In order to discover what actually happens while we are worshiping, let us each think of some outstanding worship experience in his own life. As we pause to think of some such great moment of worship, we probably realize that in that moment something vital happened to us. In other words, worship is first of all an experience. The most important thing about it is its experience quality. Worship may express itself through certain forms, but worship itself is not primarily a form; it is an experience. I may say, "I am going to morning worship," but unless *I worship,* unless I feel God's presence and my inner life of the spirit is quickened, there has been no worship for *me,* even though I have participated in certain so-called "acts of worship." We must worship "in spirit and in truth." From the standpoint of leadership, when a minister or a group leader plans a service of worship, he plans and confidently expects that something will happen to the worshipers. Someone has said that "Learning is the vital part of teaching." It is just as true that the experience of the worshiper is the vital element in worship.

What is it, then, that we expect a genuine experience of worship to do for an individual or a group?

Worship gives reality to the God companionship experience. If worship is, as we have seen, first of all an experience, this indicates that in worship the individual is changed so that he emerges from the experience in some respect a different person from the person he was before the act of worship. This change is in the direc-

14

tion of an intensified consciousness of God's presence with him, a consciousness which is strengthened during the worship experience, but which tends to go with him in the manifold other activities of his daily life.

This sense of God's presence may be only a comforting feeling of security in a changing world, or it may develop, through training in worship and practice of the presence of God, to be a real sharing of God's purposes for our own lives and for the building of a better world.

Jesus, the most radiant, the most convincing personality on the pages of the world's history, moved through his days with an unshaken confidence in a God whose purposes underlay the universe, a God with whose purposes he could unite. Jesus could be forceful and could live life creatively because of his constant sense of fellowship with a God who is himself an active, creative God. The God of Jesus is constantly represented as seeking communion with his children. Not only do they seek him, but he is ever trying to find ways to express himself to them and to share his purposes with them. In the story-pictures of Jesus, God seeks those who are lost; he rejoices over those who return to his companionship; he is a God who is seeking man as surely as man is seeking him. However modern man may think of God, he needs to recapture this unshakable belief of Jesus in a God with whom he can share a life of the spirit.

The first and most important aim of worship, then, is to strengthen in every worshiper the belief in such a God. No more poignant words could be found than those of Sidney Lanier to describe what the experience of worship may mean:

"As the marsh-hen secretly builds on the watery sod,
  Behold I will build me a nest on the greatness of God;

15

I will fly in the greatness of God as the marsh-hen flies
In the freedom that fills all the space 'twixt the marsh and the
    skies:
By so many roots as the marsh-hen sends in the sod
I will heartily lay me a-hold on the greatness of God."[2]

Worship reveals higher values. The changes which
occur during worship often result in a heightened and
surer sense of value. Not only may the worshiper discern higher values than he has hitherto recognized, but
these higher values appeal to him as being infinitely
desirable. There often attends this quickened desire for
higher values a whole set of aspirations and resolves,
accompanied by an emotional glow which renews the
worshiper's hope of ethical and spiritual achievement.

Most of us have the experience of glimpsing the
beauty and worth of ideals only to let life and its activities dim this vision. Through the illumination which
comes through worship we catch a new sense of their
significance and worth for us.

Worship brings ethical insight. The truer sense of
values which comes through worship makes possible a
clearer ethical insight, bringing the worshiper a vision
of more Christ-like attitudes to assume toward his fellow men and of more fruitful ways of living with them.
Dr. George A. Coe says:

Worship can gather together what has been and what is,
with a view to determining, both individually and socially,
what shall be; and it can do this with the greatest thorough-
ness, breadth, and poise because it includes a consciousness of
doing it with God. The worshiper can sharpen and broaden
his discriminations in one ethical area after another without
end; he can thereby check his faults, and likewise his virtues,
which always need revaluation; he can increase his sense of

---

[2] Sidney Lanier, "The Marshes of Glynn," from *Hymns of the
Marshes,* p. 57. Charles Scribner's Sons. Used by permission.

oneness with his fellows; he can acquire a habit of rejoicing in the good even when it is costly and, in his realization of God, he can acquire the spirit of unlimited adventure.[3]

Worship aids in the solution of problems. To discern higher values and to sharpen one's ethical discrimination almost inevitably involve an individual in the facing of some challenging problems. But the very worship experience which makes one more sensitive to problems often makes possible the solution of them. We come to God with problems which tax all of our powers of insight and intelligence. In worship we relax and place ourselves in a mood receptive to suggestion. We become less tense so we can view the problem objectively. We feel the need for more than our immediate strength for the solution, and gradually we begin to feel that we are not individuals struggling alone but that we are a part of the ongoing process of the universe. As such, we cannot fail. "God is working his purposes out" and we are part of that purpose. We begin to glimpse a solution to the problem which is in harmony with God's purpose for a developing world. And we begin to slough off our selfishness, our personal concern for our own interests, and we substitute an insight into the adjustment which we as individuals must make in order to solve the problem.

We must interpret "problems" to mean not only those personal difficulties which every individual has to meet, but those larger problems of social significance which can never be solved apart from an identification of ourselves with God's purposes. Professor Bennett says: "If worship is the thing I take it to be, then we

---

[3] From *What Is Christian Education?* pp. 123, 124. **Charles Scribner's Sons.** Used by permission.

should look to it to set a fresh and invigorating, if disturbing, air moving about our accepted standards. It should make for independence of mind; it should create that kind of rebel who is not only rebel but prophet as well."[4]

Worship releases spiritual energies. Through worship comes the realization of sources of strength, both within and outside ourselves, which we can draw upon to help us in our tasks. It is as though spiritual energies which had been lying dormant were suddenly released. This may be that feeling of "Vitality" of which Doctor Vogt speaks. There is a feeling of one-ness with God so that his strength and power become our own. This is true whether we think of the worship experience with the simple naïveté of the child who asks and believes that he miraculously receives, or whether we analyze the process psychologically and see how much our own response and attitude of mind bring the sense of power.

Worship renews the zest for life. It is Doctor Coe who suggests this possibility of the worship experience to us. In worship an "invigorating" air blows about the commonplace activities so that man sees life, not as something to be endured, but as a glorious adventure. In worship anxieties are relieved, fear and discouragement are removed, and the trivial takes its proper place. The worshiper tends to see life whole, with the result that enthusiasm for living is kindled. Life is not only a matter of problem-solving, of challenge and of action. It also involves experiences of appreciation and enjoyment. If worship is, as Doctor Vogt says, "a celebration of life," it must make a place for all of life's major experiences.

---

[4] *Journal of Religion*, Vol. VI, p. 499. Used by permission.

WHAT IS WORSHIP?

Worship unifies life around a central purpose. One of the greatest needs of any individual is that of finding a meaning which will unify all of life's many interests and activities. There is need of a sense of some value which will supersede all other values. We are restless and ineffectual in our living until we find such a unifying purpose. We read and talk to-day about the importance of having an "integrated personality." Many psychiatrists tell us that religion can provide that integrating force, that sense of value which gives meaning to all other values and which makes it possible for us to live with conviction and with joyful expectancy. One of the important functions of worship is to see that religion renders this service to its followers.

Worship creates a sense of fellowship with all mankind. We must never forget that worship has its social as well as its individual emphasis. Doctor Brightman calls this aspect of the worship experience "fruition in a Community of Love."[5] Worship reaches its perfection only as we have a feeling for the many, God's other children, and when our dedication is not only a dedication to God but to the brotherhood of mankind.

Worship enlists the worshiper in the building of a Christian social order. The act of worship is not complete until it has stirred the social passion of the worshiper and he sees in the "Community of Love" his opportunity to complete the "unfinished tasks of Christianity." One of the aims of the worship program should be to send the worshiper out from the moment of worship to other moments of high endeavor and enlistment in the cause of the kingdom of God. In

---

[5] Edgar Sheffield Brightman, *Religious Values*, pp. 221ff. The Abingdon Press. Used by permission.

response to the vision of new ideals which worship brings, the worshiper cries out, "Here am I; send me."

Worship establishes a pattern for what worship may be. One of the greatest values of public worship is its ability to establish a worship pattern. The individual finds it difficult to remain continuously on the highest levels of God-companionship. As one worshiper has said,

> "Isn't it strange how God is easy to forget?
> And to remember too?"

Each one of us needs frequently to have the whole experience of worship made beautiful and worthy through carefully planned services of worship. We cannot get away from the fact that the best teaching about what worship should be and as to how to worship comes through participation in meaningful worship experiences. In actual communion with God we learn *how* to have fellowship with him.

When we think of our own outstanding worship experience, we probably recognize that some of these things happened to us. In fact, if we stop to think of it, we see that the experience which we call worship is made up of, not one, but a series of experiences, including such steps as vision, contemplation, repentance, recollection, resolve, fellowship—all of these shot through with a consciousness of God.[6]

Some writers believe that worship always follows one psychological pattern, and that every service of worship should conform to that pattern. Others feel that not all of the expressions of worship necessarily occur in every worship experience, and that, while we hope that all of the purposes of worship mentioned above may be real-

---

[6] See Appendix A. "The Nature of Worship."

ized at some time in the life of every worshiper, some of them will receive greater emphasis in some services of worship than in others.

The dominant moods of worship seem to be joy, assurance and peace. But sorrow also may be present at some points in the worship experience. The worshiper may deeply regret his own lack of spiritual achievement in the light of the new vision of values which he discerns. Or he may feel deeply penitent over the social sin which is at the root of human misery.

Before closing this discussion of what goes on during worship, we ought to turn our attention away from the worshiper to God himself. Some writers describe the chief function of worship as adoration of God. We have seen how the strengthening of the tie which binds the worshiper to God is the fundamental aspect of all worship, and this chapter deals with that relationship as a mutual experience—a shared companionship of the spirit between God and man. Does the experience of worship affect God?

Many of us find it impossible to contemplate a God who enjoys a personal satisfaction in acts of praise and adoration for their own sakes. But, some say, this is not the only alternative. If God's Spirit can meet ours, must there not be experiencing on his part as well as on ours? Byington says, "Whoever worships in spirit and in truth cannot escape the conviction that God is also experiencing something."[7] Dr. George A. Coe speaks of God as a social being and says, "God as well as man is a social being. Glorifying him, accordingly, is no interplay between two individuals, each of whom

---

[7] *The Quest for Experience in Worship*, p. 172. Harper and Brothers.

seeks his own particular ends, but, rather, the maintenance of such an intimate relationship between the human and the divine existence as enables each to realize his life in the life of the other."[8]

SOME VARYING ASPECTS OF WORSHIP

If we are to help childhood and youth and adult life to have a genuine experience of God, we must understand what are some of the forms which the worship experience may take. In our attempt to see the problem clearly, it may help us to look at some varying aspects of worship.

Uttered or Unexpressed Worship. One of our hymns says that

> "Prayer is the soul's sincere desire,
> Uttered or unexpressed."

Undoubtedly all of us can look back to some moments in our lives when we have been under the spell of a great moment of worship, but when for one reason or another expression was impossible. On the Gorner Gratz, opposite the Matterhorn, I caught my first vision of a world of glaciers and gleaming snow peaks. Nothing but blinding, dazzling whiteness anywhere except the little shoulder of land on which my friends and I stood. Heaven above and a world of untouched purity. In that moment God seemed to be saying: "Behold, I make all things new! Creation lies ahead, not behind. Every day is a fresh beginning. Every morn is the world made new. Walk ye, therefore, in newness of life." All of worship was there in those brief few moments of wonder. Yet not a word was said and never

---

[8] *The Religion of a Mature Mind,* by George Albert Coe, p. 184. Fleming H. Revell Company, publishers, New York. Used by permission.

was the experience even mentioned until years afterward.

However, it is probable that that moment was made possible, at least in part, by years of expressed worship on Sunday mornings. And, after all, though not a word was said, there *was* an expression—an outpouring of the self to God, the Maker and Creator of all things new.

Spontaneous and Induced Worship. The previous experience of worship was spontaneous. No one had planned the setting with the purpose of stimulating a worship experience. Once again on that same trip I stood one day in the aisle of Westminster Abbey. I had slipped away from my fellow travelers for a moment to be alone and to sense the beauty around me. Suddenly as I stood there a voice whispered, "Look at your feet," and the tactful leader of the party, after his whispered suggestion, as quickly slipped away and left me to my solitude. I looked down and there, right at my feet in the marble floor, was a tablet bearing that famous inscription:

BROUGHT BY FAITHFUL HANDS
OVER LAND AND SEA
HERE RESTS
DAVID LIVINGSTONE
MISSIONARY, TRAVELER, PHILANTHROPIST

And there amid the columns and stained-glass windows of the great Abbey came one of those mystical moments of communion with David Livingstone's God and with Livingstone and other heroes of the faith. For a brief few moments I was "encompassed by so great a cloud of witnesses."

The following Sunday I took my place in the pews in the same great Abbey along with hundreds of other worshipers, when the experience of worship was stimulated by organ music, the processional of robed choirs, and the beautiful ritual of the Church of England. In the spontaneous outreach of the spirit after God, alone with the spirit of David Livingstone, there had been real worship. It was more spontaneous in character than the experience induced by the formal church service, in that it sprang up in response to no planned stimuli. Yet we must note that in the first instance a wise and understanding leader took advantage of the opportunity he saw to bring to fruition a spontaneous worship feeling. In many classroom periods there may suddenly develop out of mutual discussion, out of new visions of truth apprehended, such spontaneous expressions of worship. Happy is that teacher who senses this spontaneous worship feeling and knows how to bring it to fruition and make an opportunity for its adequate expression!

Individual and Social Worship. There is another contrast in worship which demands our attention. That is the alternating emphasis upon the individual's personal relationship to God and his consciousness of being part of a larger group. This differentiation may have two meanings. It may indicate that worship in which the individual participates when alone as over against the worship in which he joins with a group. There is another significance to the terms, however. One individual in his *personal* devotions may be socially minded and carry the needs of a world of men in his communion with God, while another person may be worshiping with a *group* and yet fail to be concerned in any real way with other needs than his own. It may be said by some that such a person is not really worshiping. Perhaps he is worshiping but with limitations.

Worship an Inhibited or a Growing Experience. It becomes evident from the foregoing that worship is or may be a growing experience. If at the heart of it there is companionship with God, the experience lays itself open to the same modifications to which any friendship is subject. Like a human friendship this companionship with God may be a sudden and vivid thing and then lose its vitality because of changed relationships. It may have a promising beginning and then die out for want of cultivation. It may never become the rich, vital experience it might be, owing to the lack of training all along the way.

The desirable type of spiritual development for any individual would include guidance through a growing experience of worship beginning with early childhood and continuing through adult life.

Worship as Form or as Experience. Different writers upon worship emphasize different aspects of it. Some put the emphasis upon worship as form. Dr. Von Ogden Vogt says, "It is primarily the form of worship rather than its content which is the chief source of the vitality of the experience and hence of its high enjoyment."[9] In another place he says, "Do you mean to say (the objector asks) that a sense of the peace of God is a derivation of some outer formal physical influence rather than of the spirit? I do mean to say something very like that, and the same concerning other religious feelings."[10] However, Mr. Vogt also remarks later, "Possibly some will always regard as ends what others designate as means."

---

[9] Reprinted by permission from *Modern Worship*, p. 13, by Von Ogden Vogt. Published by Yale University Press.
[10] *Ibid.*, pp. 15-16.

Certainly for some the content of worship takes first place in importance as a basis for a genuine worship experience. For these the ideas of God and of our relation to him which a worship service contains may entirely prohibit any real experience of worship, no matter how perfect the form of the service. Others are not so easily influenced by content. For them "it is the formal element rather than the content which is chiefly the source of the vitality and enjoyment of worship."[11]

But wherever we place the emphasis, we are all agreed that the content of worship is important, and we all recognize that lack of attention to form has been one of the serious defects in worship, especially as it has been planned for groups in the church school. The problems confronting us in these pages concern themselves with the ways in which we can enrich the content of worship and beautify and perfect its form of expression for different age-groups of worshipers.

Formal and Informal Worship. The devotional life, for most of us, seeks expression in two ways. We respond to the enactment of the presence of God through ritual and liturgy; our worship feelings are stimulated by beautiful and carefully-thought-out forms. But we also crave the expression of our spirit of worship in less formal ways—in family groups about the hearth, in a mid-week prayer meeting, at the sunset hour on a hillside overlooking a lake, or in a discussion group in an upper room on a Sunday morning. The setting for such informal worship experiences varies, and there are many gradations in the amount of informality.

Such informal worship experiences need not lack in beauty or even dignity. Informality is not to be con-

[11] *Ibid.*, p. 19.

fused with carelessness in either the planning or the conduct of such services. An informal service of worship often requires as much if not more planning than one of the formal type. There are times when its informal character depends upon the participating of a number of people, which complicates the task of preparation. It is an achievement of a high order to plan and conduct such informal worship experiences so as to maintain a dominant worshipful mood. But the value of such informal expressions of worship lies in the extension of the practice of the presence of God to many situations in life.

Adult and Child Worship. There is one more differentiation which we may make in our analysis of the problem of worship. Certainly it is evident to all, in this day of the understanding of human psychology and social heredity and environment, *that at different stages of our development we bring to worship a different experience*. And if worship is to be vital, it must meet the needs of that experience in which the individual finds himself. The little child with his first wondering questions about God and the world around him needs a certain type of worship. The adolescent, with just enough contacts with life to raise many questions about its possibilities, facing the task of adjustment to his lifework and the normal development of newly awakened desires, needs another type of worship. The adult actively engaged in business or professional life, or the adult denied this opportunity for self-expression, the adult forced to face the complex problems of the world to-day, must, through worship, find help for these adult needs. These differences in experience and age will affect both the content and the form of worship.

GUIDING THE EXPERIENCE OF WORSHIP

By all the problems of worship suggested in this chapter, by the possibilities of the enrichment of life which we have seen worship to offer, by the necessity of a God-relationship in every life if lives are to reach the heights of Jesus' way of living, by the universal need of God, we are called as leaders in religious education to help make possible for every individual his right to a God-conscious life.

Over a thousand years ago one of India's poets uttered this cry:

> "The sound of a sob in the darkness,
>   A child crieth after its Father.
> My spirit within me is burning,
>   Consumed with passionate yearning,
> O unknown, far away Father!
> No voice answers out of the darkness."

As leaders in religious education we are called to see that through a genuine experience of worship a Voice answers to every child and youth and adult, "If he calls upon me, I will answer him."

ADDITIONAL READING SOURCES

Brightman, Edgar Sheffield, *Religious Values*. The Abingdon Press. Chaps. VII-IX.

Byington, Edwin H., *The Quest for Experience in Worship*. Harper & Brothers.

Cabot, Richard, *What Men Live By*. Part IV. Houghton Mifflin Company.

Dearmer, Percy, *The Art of Public Worship*. Morehouse Publishing Company.

Fiske, George Walter, *The Recovery of Worship*. The Macmillan Company.

Harris, Thomas L., *Christian Public Worship*. Harper & Brothers.

Hill, Mabel (Ed.), *Wise Men Worship*. E. P. Dutton & Co.

Jones, Rufus, *Studies in Mystical Religion*. The Macmillan Company.

WHAT IS WORSHIP?

Odgers, J. Hastie, and Schutz, Edward G., *The Technique of Public Worship*. The Methodist Book Concern.

Parker, F. S., *Practice and Experience of Christian Worship*. Cokesbury Press.

Religious Education, October, 1925, "A Symposium on Worship" (article).

Ross, G. A. Johnston, *Christian Worship and Its Future*. The Abingdon Press.

Sclater, J. R. P., *The Public Worship of God*. Harper & Brothers.

Soares, Theodore G., *Religious Education*. Chaps. XIV and XV. University of Chicago Press.

Sperry, Willard L., *Reality in Worship*. The Macmillan Company.

Streeter, Burnett Hillman, *Reality*. The Macmillan Company.

Vogt, Von Ogden, *Modern Worship*. Yale University Press.

Wieman, Henry Nelson, *Methods of Private Religious Living*. The Macmillan Company.

Wieman, Henry Nelson, *The Wrestle of Religion With Truth*. Chaps. III-VII. The Macmillan Company.

CHAPTER II

AIDS TO WORSHIP

On desert sands the vision comes,
    As men turn towards the east,
And while some fasting see God's face,
    Some find him at the feast.

The Ancients found him in their groves,
    The Wise Men saw the star,
He comes to some in paths of peace,
    To some in flaming war.

Wherever man has fought for right,
    Where man for man has died;
Beside him stands, could we but see,
    One that was crucified.

In temples and cathedral dim,
    Through vigil, chant, and prayer,
Wherever man cries out to God,
    The Living God is there.

            —HINTON WHITE.[1]

WORSHIP comes to its most perfect expression under certain conditions of environment or in situations where certain laws are operating, or in response to certain experiences. The one who is to plan worship programs must be something of a scientist and also of an artist as well as a religionist. He is a practical scientist in so far as he understands the psychological laws underlying the worship experience and definitely plans to use these laws in order to stimulate worship. But he is also a creative artist in that he is attempting to express an

---

[1] Book source unknown to author.

inner spiritual reality in a form that is emotionally satisfying.

Let us see if we can discover what are some of the situations and conditions which make worship possible.

THE SENSE OF NEED AS AN AID TO WORSHIP

Sometimes the worshiper comes to the worship service with a conscious sense of need. He longs to find his need met in worship. It is a recognized fact in the educational world that any new experience will yield a more fruitful return if the individual has an appetite for it, if he comes to it with a sense of personal concern. One of the problems of worship is to stimulate this feeling of need or to make conscious to the worshiper his rather vague feeling after God.

Worship Closely Related to Experience. This feeling that he needs the help which worship can give will come in proportion to the degree in which the worship service is related to the worshiper's everyday life experiences or his present interests and needs. If worship never touches the real problems of the group that is worshiping, it is like seed falling on ground not ready for it. When worship grows out of the life experiences of the worshiping group, it not only meets real needs but reveals to the group a consciousness of what its spiritual needs are.

The Need to Share Jesus' Experience of Worship. We have seen in Chapter I how Jesus' trusting confidence in a God whose companionship he could share made it possible for him to live his life courageously and radiantly. It also gave direction to all his efforts, purpose to all his dreams, and creative energy to achieve his purpose, no matter to what lengths of sacrifice it might lead him. There never was a time in the history of the world when men so needed to share this experience of Jesus.

THE INFLUENCE OF ENVIRONMENT

Most of us are aware that in certain environments we are more likely to worship than in others. In every case it would not be possible to put our finger upon just the environmental characteristics which are responsible for stimulating or encouraging the worship experience. But we can pick out certain aspects of environment which often will be conducive to worship.

Relation Between the Æsthetic Feelings and the Religious Feelings. From the earliest time art and religion have gone hand in hand. Percy Dearmer says: "Art, we believe, cannot be understood unless it is realized as a part of life as a whole, and especially of religion."[2] We can all testify in our own experience to the sweep of religious feeling and the awareness of God which often come to us in the presence of overwhelming beauty. Why this is so, is a matter for a course in the psychology of the æsthetic feelings. We are concerned here with its clear implications for worship.

Beauty in Environment. One implication is that beauty of environment is an aid to worship. There are different forms in which this beauty may manifest itself. There is first of all the beauty which reveals itself in structure, line, and form. Our Protestant churches are recognizing the need for worshipful buildings if we are to raise a generation of worshipers. There is beauty in

[2] *The Necessity of Art*, Preface, pp. v and vi. Student Christian Movement, London, England.

the fitness of the environment for the experiences of worship.

Not only for adults, but for children and young people are needed worshipful rooms. Some churches are building departmental rooms that in some respects resemble chapels, which by their architecture suggest worship. Other churches are fortunate enough to have one very beautiful chapel which is used on Sundays by three or four alternating groups in the church school. But, let us remember that the Gothic chapel, or the formal chapel of any type, is not the only environment in which people can worship. In fact, it would be unfortunate if children and young people should get the idea that worship in any other setting than a church or chapel is impossible. Little children who are learning to worship need a homelike, informal environment, which will not overawe them but which will help them to be spontaneous and natural in their expressions of worship as they are in all their other activities. In young people's groups there is a place for the informal expression of worship around an open fireplace or beside a lake as well as for expression in a churchly setting.

Churches that are planning to build new educational plants should consult with children's workers who understand the type of room which is suitable for the worship of children and who have experimented with different types of worship environments for children.

There are many who feel that Gothic architecture is pre-eminently the most aspiring, worshipful form. And it is true that its groined arches, its tall columns, its aspiring lines tend to carry the spirit Godward. But there is a sweetness and simplicity as well as an austerity of line about a rural New England church which also

speaks of God. In writing about a country church one
poet says:

"I think God seeks this house, serenely white,
  Upon this hushed, elm-bordered street, as one
With many mansions seeks, in calm delight,
  A boyhood cottage intimate with sun.
I think God feels himself the owner here,
  Not just rich Host to some self-seeking throng,
But Friend of village folk who want him near
  And offer him simplicity and song.

"No stained-glass windows hide the world from view;
  And it is well. The world is lovely there
Beyond clear panes where branch-scrolled skies look through
  And fields and hills, in morning hours of prayer.

"God spent his youth with field and hill and tree,
  And Christ grew up in rural Galilee."[3]

Beauty of coloring, as well as beauty of structure, is
an aid to worship. For many church schools which do
not have rooms designed especially for worship, beauty
of color is possible. In a chapel or church we get beautiful colors in stained-glass windows, stone and woodwork, choir gowns, and emblems.

But all of us, even though we do not have chapels,
can have rooms that are tinted in soft and pleasing
colors which suggest light and vitality. Walls can be
toned to harmonize with woodwork. Gray walls do not
belong to dark brown woodwork. There are some colors
which are drab and depressing. Cold grays and yellow-
greens may not show soil, but they are apt to suggest
dinginess and to depress the spirit. Walls, woodwork,
furniture, rugs, draperies should all harmonize. The
taste of those who understand colors and interior

---

[3] "A Country Church," by Violet Allen Storey, in *Good Housekeeping,* September, 1926. D. Appleton-Century Company. Used by
permission.

decorating should be consulted. If a room must be used for worship as well as for other departmental purposes, certain color combinations are better than others.

All of us may have the *beauty of cleanliness and orderliness*. There is no excuse for a dirty, dusty church building so long as there are soap and water, and boys and girls who, under direction, can make rooms and furniture clean, if there is no other way of having it done. As far as possible the room should present an appearance of freshness and orderliness, with no wraps lying around in conspicuous places, or no ill-assorted piles of unused hymnals to offend the eye.

Enriching the Environment of Worship. A room may be made beautiful for worship by the introduction of beautiful accessories. Pictures which suggest worship, a growing plant, a bowl of flowers, branches of vivid autumn leaves, flags and emblems, all of these may contribute to the environment of worship.

This environment should be rich enough in beauty to stimulate the imagination of the worshiper and yet not so profuse with stimulating objects as to stifle imagination. A wall covered with pictures will focus the attention on nothing in particular. Only confusion and bewilderment are produced. A few pictures, well chosen, a few objects artistically arranged, give the worshiper the opportunity really to appreciate and enjoy the beauty.

Sometimes it is desirable to create a focus for the attention of the worshiper, a central point of beauty. Often the effect of an altar can be created by a table with a beautiful worship picture hanging over it and with candlesticks at each end of the table, or a low bowl holding a few flowers. Simplicity should be the keynote.

There are churches which sense the inadequacy of

their church environment for worship, but which feel that the expense of renovation would be prohibitive. This is not necessarily so. An unattractive room can be transformed into a beautiful room for worship by the erection of a simple altar and a few other touches, and this with the expenditure of a very little money.

In many churches there are young people and adults who, under supervision, could contribute their services for labor in carpentry, painting, and sewing to make such a project perfectly possible.

Is Beauty Essential? There have been periods in the history of Protestantism when beauty has been looked upon with suspicion or banned entirely. There have been and are wide differences in the attitudes of worshiping groups as to the most perfect setting for worship. The severe simplicity of the Quaker meeting house represents the ideal of one group, while at the opposite pole we have the richness of the Gothic cathedral. The fact that we have two such opposite points of view and others all along the way between, suggests the individual differences in people and the need to provide for such differences as we plan both the form and the setting of worship.

Beauty has power to put the individual into a mood of relaxation, of appreciation, of utter surrender to all the influences of worship. Children and adolescents are sensitive to beauty and often respond to its subtle influence with moods of extreme suggestibility to ideal values.

There are those who fear that if beauty of environment is overemphasized, there is a danger that in our worship we shall be content to substitute the emotional response to beauty for a fellowship with God, or that we shall let beauty drug our spirits with content with things as they are. The contention is sometimes made that the most ritualistic churches are those with the least social vision, and churches have been criticized recently for putting millions of dollars into elaborate edifices for worship while people starve outside the church doors. The following poem expresses the revolt of this group of people:

"To a Prince of the Church[4]

"The vestments in your church, they say,
   Are rich with dyes and stiff with gold;
A thousand miners' kids to-day
   Hide in their shanties from the cold.

"That chalice—gift of loving pride—
   The gems blaze as you lift it up;
A thousand babies, solemn-eyed,
   Click spoons within an empty cup.

"So might I sling the sneering stone.
   But God will judge both me and you;
You sin not, nor are judged, alone.
   I had two coats; *I still have two.*"

Both of these points of view are important and need consideration. It does not seem necessary to take an extreme position. Beauty has its religious uses, and if we recognize the dangers of overemphasis, we can use beauty as one of God's gifts. Winfred Garrison says, "God as artist has been working through the ages with the media of things and sounds and colors, filling the world with a beauty which is biologically superfluous but spiritually necessary, bodying forth his thought in forms and hues and materials, most of all working with this highly plastic yet strangely resistant human material, as we do with our children, to make a product which shall have an eternal worth of its own and shall

---

[4] Kenneth W. Porter, in *Poems of Justice*, p. 115.

be an expression of the spiritual realities which lie at the heart of the universe. Man has no higher privilege than that of being like him, an artist both appreciative and creative."[5]

But, while we recognize the power of beauty, we must, at the same time, realize that some of life's greatest worship experiences can and do occur in situations that are bleak or ugly—that there are other influences besides that of beauty which "stab our spirits wide awake" and challenge us to worship. In the presence of human misery men cry out to God and dedicate themselves anew to the fruition of worship in a "Community of Love."[6]

SYMBOLISM IN THE WORSHIP ENVIRONMENT

Someone has said that art came into existence to say the things which words could not say. It is true that the greatest truths cannot be adequately expressed in words. The poet may use words, but it is the language of symbolism upon which he falls back to utter for us those unutterable truths which we feel but are too inarticulate to express.

For this reason symbolism, if it is the expression in art form of great experiences and truths, may stimulate the imagination of the worshiper and help him to recall in his moments of recollection the heights of spiritual truth which mankind has reached in the past or toward which he is aspiring in the present. There was a day when the Christian symbols were representations of present and living truth. Those symbolical decorations in the catacombs were the reminders of a present faith.

---

[5] In *Affirmative Religion*, p. 208. Harper & Brothers. Used by permission.
[6] Edgar Sheffield Brightman, in *Religious Values*. The Abingdon Press. Used by permission.

AIDS TO WORSHIP

There is a growing feeling to-day that our modern churches should, through their plastic art and stained-glass windows, suggest to the worshiping group the religious significance of the daily concerns of men of our own day.

It is true that we enter the house of worship to forget for a while the affairs of daily living. However, we seek to forget them for a moment, only to wish to recall them again, but to recall them with a new feeling of their desirability or their possible worth to us. Why should not the workingman see in the symbols of beauty around him suggestions of the dignity of labor so that he might return to his work after the hour of worship conscious of a partnership with God as he feels, "My Father worketh hitherto and I work"? Why should not the child see carved in stone and wrought in jeweled glass symbols of that play life in which he delights, so that he might whisper to himself, "And the streets of the city shall be full of boys and girls playing in the streets thereof"? Why should not the youth find a new meaning in his scholastic effort and teachers, physicians, scientists, philosophers, artists, see symbols of their vocations suggesting that all these may help to enrich the religious life of man and that the religious motive may make every profession minister to that "more abundant life"?[7]

Wonder as a Basis for Worship

The worship of primitive man was closely associated

---

[7] Some examples of the use of symbolism to interpret present-day interests are the following:
    The Athletic Window, Cathedral of Saint John the Divine.
    Sculpture, University of Chicago Chapel.
    Stained-Glass Windows, Trinity Methodist Church, Springfield, Massachusetts.
    First Unitarian Church, Chicago, Illinois.
    Saint John's Reformed Church School, Lansdale, Penna.

with his awe in the presence of natural forces which he did not understand or wonder at the beauty or power he sensed around him. The Psalmist expressed this wonder at God's majesty and power when he said:

> "Wonderful are thy works;
> And that my soul knoweth right well."

In much of our modern worship there may be this same feeling of wonder, for we can never get away from the miracle of life.

In planning worship services we can consciously induce the attitude of worship by appealing to the sense of wonder. In spite of—no, because of—the discoveries of modern science, the marvels of nature astound us. When we hear about the universe full of star-worlds so many millions of light years away from our earth, our minds are stretched to infinite efforts at comprehension of the power or law back of such wonders. When, on the silver screen we watch exquisite flowers slowly unfolding their lovely petals to reveal hearts of gold and realize that this manifestation of beauty is going on all around us in the woods and fields day after day, we feel with Tennyson:

> "Flower in the crannied wall,
> I pluck you out of the crannies;
> I hold you here, root and all, in my hand,
> Little flower—but *if* I could understand
> What you are, root and all, and all in all,
> I should know what God and man is."

There is a wonder too born of the hearing about heroic acts of living. The adventures of the great heroes of the faith stimulate in all of us new wonder at the possibilities of divine living in human personalities. "The stars in heaven are not so grand as a man living in obedience to the higher law, or dying when it is better not to live."[8] It is well for childhood and youth not to lose the ability to wonder at the beauty and grandeur of life. For it is in those moments of wonder that we apprehend the majesty of God in life. But it is equally important that adults living in a world that questions everything, that analyzes, that criticizes and that evaluates, should still retain the sense of wonder at the eternal mysteries, for

> "He who keeps through all his days
> Open eyes of wonder
> Is the lord of skiey ways
> And the earth thereunder."[9]

APPRECIATION AS A CONDITION OF WORSHIP

Many people lose much of the power of worship because they fail to appreciate the meaning of the worship materials or their relationship to the worshiper's experience. Also people often do not see the significance of the forms in which worship is clothed. A definite program of education for worship which emphasizes the appreciation of worship materials will reveal possibilities in worship hitherto unguessed.

Appreciation in Child Experience. The public schools are laying great emphasis upon lessons in music appreciation, art appreciation, and appreciation of literature. A group of children who have been led through an appreciation lesson on Millet's picture, "The Angelus," and have associated with it Gounod's "L'Angelus," when they hear the music played in their worship service, will not only listen attentively but will be prepared to enter with genuine participation into a service of

---

[8] Quoted by Von Ogden Vogt, in *Modern Worship*, p. 82.
[9] Wilfred Gibson.

worship on the themes of gratitude or prayer. Without this appreciation lesson certain parts of the worship service would be far less meaningful to them.

Hymns, prayers, and Scripture gain a power and vitality when we have first been led to study them for an understanding of their meanings and an appreciation of their beauty and their significance in the worship service as well as for life. Sometimes the story of the artist or composer or poet will make a selection glow with beauty. Sometimes an incident revealing what a certain selection has meant in the lives of others gives it new power over our own lives.

Adults need less stimulation of the appreciation faculty than do children because of their richer background of experience. Whatever fullness of life we bring to any situation determines what we get out of it. Appreciation depends in part upon the number and strength of the associations we have built up around any concept. The music, the hymns, the responses of any worship service call up more associations in the consciousness of adults than of children, because older people have a richer experience, as a rule. This is one reason why there should be definite planning for appreciation periods as a preparation for worship with children and young people.[10]

Appreciation in Adult Experience. Yet, even adults need such preparation too. For there are great differences in the backgrounds of older people. As an illustration of this fact that we tend to enjoy the familiar things around which we have built up associations, witness the reluctance of adults and of many young people's groups to try a new hymn. The old familiar words and

---

[10] See Chap. X, "Preparation for Worship."

tunes are sung with enthusiasm; a new one, chosen for its remarkable fitness for a certain worship service, may fail to meet with a response.

One church when it bought new hymnals, sent for the editor of that hymnal, who used the period of a Sunday-morning service to lead the adult congregation to an appreciation of its contents and form. He helped them to appreciate new types of hymns, new content for a new age, the form in which the hymnal was arranged. Then, he studied with them certain hymn tunes and words, revealing to them a richness of beauty and meaning of which they had not been conscious and enlisting their co-operation in the adventure of a growing worship experience based upon an appreciation of the materials of worship.

Solitude as a Condition of Worship

There are times when being alone helps us to worship. Harriet Beecher Stowe wrote:

"Alone with thee, amid the mystic shadows,
    The solemn hush of nature newly born;
Alone with thee in breathless adoration,
    In the calm dew and freshness of the morn."

One reason why we so often feel worshipful when we are in God's great outdoors is because, even though we may be with others, there is a feeling in the open spaces that we are alone with God. For this reason there is great value in services of worship held out-of-doors. Workers with young people in summer camps have seen young people worship as they never seem to in their home churches.

The Feeling of Solitude in the Church Environment.

This feeling of being alone with God can be created even in a church environment if that environment suggests something different from the outside world, so that we have a feeling of temporarily leaving behind the complex interests and problems of life when we enter. For this reason the environment of worship should suggest simplicity. All distractions should be removed, all suggestions to the eye and ear of things which only call the attention away from worship. Interruptions from visitors or late-comers should be jealously avoided, so that the worshiper may have a chance to feel that "no one walks the way with me but God."

Though simplicity of environment will help to create this feeling of solitude, the surroundings should not be bare, but should contain enough in the way of beauty and suggestion to stimulate the imagination with worshipful content.

GROUP-CONSCIOUSNESS AS AN AID TO WORSHIP

Rhythm is a form used in all the arts, and one of the rhythmic alternations which we need in worship is the shifting emphasis upon the One and the Many. We are alone with God, yet we are conscious of ourselves as members of a great group of God-conscious worshipers, each alone with God, yet all "bound together in the bundle of life." The psychology of group feeling helps us to understand this. There is a power in a shared experience. As Saint Augustine said, "One loving spirit sets another on fire."

THE ATMOSPHERE OF WORSHIP

In order to dissolve the word "atmosphere" from its vagueness of meaning into concrete and tangible expressions, let us consider some of the qualities of which it is made.

Atmosphere of Quiet. First, an atmosphere of quiet is essential for worship. This is created by restful, harmonious colors, by the arrangement of the room, by organ or piano music played as the worshipers enter, and by the suggestion of quiet in the manner of those leading worship. A beautiful church building often carries its own suggestion of quiet.

The power of suggestion is strong in creating attitudes and determining atmosphere. This is especially true with children and young people. There is the story of a visitor to a certain schoolroom who was greatly impressed with the politeness of the pupils. He inquired of one boy, "What does your teacher do to make you so polite?"

"Oh, I don't know," replied the boy. "She just walks around and we feel as polite as anything."[11]

So, quiet, poise, relaxation may be suggested by the manner of the leader and teachers, and choir members.

The atmosphere of quiet should not be oppressive nor suggest deadness or inertia. There is such a thing as power and vitality and life without confusion or noise. Children and young people crave this feeling of vitality. The leader's manner should suggest repose and quietness of spirit, combined with happiness and expectancy.

An Atmosphere of Happiness. An atmosphere of happiness is also conducive to worship. In the church-school department where problems of discipline and of "keeping order" are pressing, there is a sense of strain which prevents whole-hearted participation in worship.

[11] Henry Churchill King, *The Moral and Religious Challenge of Our Times,* p. 307. The Macmillan Company, New York. Used by permission.

Sometimes boys and girls come to church school smarting with a sense of injustice because of some home situation or vividly unhappy because of wishes thwarted. Mary, who is in the Intermediate Department, has had an argument with her mother, who wants her to wear her dark-blue skirt. Mary says it is all wrinkled down the back and "everyone will notice it." There is not time to press it before she leaves and she wants to wear her new light-green dress. Mother says she must save it for the graduating party, and anyway it is not an appropriate dress to wear to church. Mary declares she will stay home rather than wear "that wrinkled old skirt." Mother insists that Mary go. And Mary, who is not an openly rebellious girl, goes. She wears the blue skirt, vividly conscious of those wrinkles and sure that "everyone" else is also. In what condition is Mary when she arrives at church to enter into a worship service? Or, John, who wanted to ride his bicycle to church and had an argument about it with his father? How ready for worship is Lois, who is the only girl in her class of senior high-school girls who was not invited by a boy to the party the night before? All the other girls are talking about the good time they had.

Or, here is a department of young people. In the group on a Sunday morning are some who are strangers in the community; some who are attacking their first jobs and finding it hard to make both ends meet; some who are not sure they have found their right place in life; some who are facing the problem of the desire for a home and marriage which must be indefinitely postponed.

Adults too are sensitive to atmosphere. In a church where people seem cold and where social distinctions have crept in to dispel a sense of fellowship, adult worshipers will find it difficult to surrender themselves to a genuine experience of worship.

For all these would-be worshipers, somehow, some way, an atmosphere that suggests happiness must be created before they are sufficiently free from their "strains in consciousness" to relax and give themselves up to the influence of worship.

All of this points to the need of a period of preparation for worship, where attitudes which will help the individuals to worship may be stimulated. Teachers in pre-session periods may do a great deal to meet this need, as they help to solve difficulties and to enlist the interest of the group in activities outside themselves, thus helping them to forget personal grievances and to be ready to throw themselves more unreservedly into the experience of worship.

An Atmosphere of Mutual Trust and the Sharing of Common Ideals. Worship flowers best in an atmosphere where we are conscious of common purposes and common tasks. If the group does not feel that it is strongly bound together, genuine worship is difficult to achieve. This is one reason for the necessity of getting departments together at some time other than the worship period, when we can discuss our ideals, share our problems as well as our separate interests, and build some plans for enterprises in which we are all to share. There should be sufficient common interests between all the classes in any one department so that when we meet for worship we have that feeling of one-ness. When we are carrying out some common task and encountering common difficulties in the accomplishment of the task, we all together arrive at moments when worship is necessary. The only way out is to take the matter to God. When worship thus grows out of our group experience and need of God, it reaches its fullest expression.

This need reveals how closely the total character of church life is related to its worship program. Manifestly, in those churches in which the members are vividly conscious of their community of purpose, there is a greater possibility of an enriching worship experience.

The Attitude of Expectancy. Inertia, due to lack of interest, will prove an insuperable obstacle to a fruitful worship experience. When a worshiping group is alive with anticipation, this very mood of expectancy opens the channels for the inpouring of God's Spirit. One way in which expectancy is built up in any group is by helping its members to enjoy satisfying worship experiences. If worship services are planned to meet their needs and interests, if they meet the deep longings of the human spirit for fellowship with God, if they are kept vital by variety in content and form,[12] gradually the worshipers come to anticipate the opportunities for worship. Later chapters will deal with the use of the opening part of the worship service[13] as one means of arousing expectancy, and of the ways in which the period of preparation for worship may arouse anticipation.[14]

An Atmosphere of Reverence. Of all the qualities of atmosphere conditioning worship the one we hear stressed oftenest is that of *reverence*. I am inclined to think that reverence, as an attitude of the worshiper, comes as one of the by-products of many of these other qualities. If there is an atmosphere of quiet and happi-

[12] See Chap. V.
[13] See Chap. V.
[14] See Chap. X.

ness and of mutual trust; if we are happily working together in a group on some worthy tasks in which we are all actively participating; if the environment in which we worship is beautiful and orderly and we are happy to be there; if we have been led to an appreciation of the worship service so that all its parts have significance for us; if those who lead us are reverent in attitude, then reverence follows. Reverence has its roots in respect and admiration for other people, for the wonder of life, for the world around us. It comes then, best, not by direct but by indirect teaching.

THE NECESSITY OF GRADED WORSHIP MATERIALS

If worship is to meet the real needs of people of different ages, the materials of worship must be different for the different age groups. The life problems of the primary child are not those of the junior high-school student. The world of the senior high-school pupil differs from that of the ten or eleven-year-old. The kindergarten child is removed from even the primary child, a few years older, by his need of adjustment to a vastly different world and by his capacity to make that adjustment. Our need of God changes as we grow and our world enlarges and our problems of living shift and change. Therefore, if worship is to be vital and really meet our needs, we must adapt our worship program for the different ages in the church school.

Graded Worship Groups in Specially Planned Rooms. The logical outcome is that the church must provide separate worship rooms for each department or grade. The character of these rooms may vary if we are to include pictures and emblems which relate to group interests. In some cases one chapel may be used at different periods by different groups, if it is rich enough in beauty to have a universal appeal. The important thing is that we shall have a place where groups can meet for graded worship and that we shall remember that even age groups that are close together, like the junior and senior high-school groups, are yet divided by differences in interests, attitudes, and everyday experience. So, combining two such age groups near each other in years may deprive them of the fullest possible benefit from worship.

This is the problem which confronts those who organize junior-church congregations made up of children from the kindergarten through the junior and sometimes the intermediate departments. Over and over again these leaders state their problem of how to find materials of worship that will hold the interest of and meet the needs of this entire group. Other leaders, who by the power of their own personalities apparently are able to hold the interest of such a widely diffused age group, fail to comprehend that while interest may be there, the real problems of living are not being met.

Shall different ages never worship together? Having stated clearly the necessity for graded worship, let us recognize that there is real value in some shared worship experiences. There are some problems common to childhood and youth, some occasions for worship when adults and children can meet together with a common purpose and ideal.

With all our emphasis upon the necessity for graded experience, there is a real danger that we shall make the cleavage between childhood and adult interests too sharp and deprive the old and young of a delightful companionship together. The way to solve this problem is not to bring children into the adult worship service every Sunday morning, when most of the worship materials have been selected for adult needs and when, often, the minister preaches a children's sermon whose subtle implications for the adult congregation far out-weigh its effectiveness in meeting boy-and-girl needs. This type of worship service does not provide that real sharing of a religious experience which results when a service of worship has been planned to meet the inter-ests and needs which are common to adults and children alike.

When worship is so planned it can be full of meaning if the leader of worship will seek to discover what are the common elements in the experiences that are shared by all and build the worship service around those com-mon elements. Then he must plan a form of worship which shall seem worthy and satisfying to the adult wor-shiper but which shall be a form in which the youngest child can participate with appreciation. Such services require hours and weeks of planning before they are ready for use.

Christmas has in it different meanings for different ages, and a combined Christmas celebration should not exclude some group celebrations where the meanings pertinent to that group are revealed. But, the Christ-mas festival has some meanings which we all share, and the whole experience of Christmas may be enriched for all ages when these common meanings are celebrated together. So it is with Easter and other great church festivals. And this is also true of such problems as world-peace and Christian citizenship, which are com-mon problems to-day to adults and children. While each group needs some worship approaches particularly from its own point of view, there may come great values from the consciousness that all of us, old and young, belong to God's family and are working and praying together for the kingdom of God.

Many small churches find it necessary to throw several age groups together for worship, because there is only one room in which to meet or because the numbers are so few that too close a grading would be impracticable. To plan worship for such groups is always more difficult, because of the wide divergence in ages, and because, if the members of the group are really to worship, the leader must build the service on interests and needs which are common to *all* in the group.

However, the understanding leader will recognize in such a situation the elements which may become real assets. Knowing that there are some results which cannot be achieved, he will definitely plan to make the most of the more intimate fellowship inherent in a small group and the possibility of strengthening the bond between old and young.

To discover adequately the psychological bases for worship would require far more space than this one chapter. But if these suggestions raise questions about existing conditions, if they open up possibilities of improvement, if they stimulate a desire to use more effectively these aids to worship, their purpose will have been realized.

ADDITIONAL READING SOURCES

Ames, Edward S., *The Psychology of Religious Experience.* Houghton Mifflin Co.

Coe, George A., *The Psychology of Religion.* University of Chicago Press.

Conover, Elbert M., *Building the House of God.* The Methodist Book Concern.

AIDS TO WORSHIP

Garrison, Winfred E., *Affirmative Religion*, Chap. XIII, "The Necessity of Art." Harper & Brothers.

Hollis, Gertrude, *Every Child's Book About the Church*. Morehouse Publishing Co.

Jones, Rufus, *Finding the Trail of Life*, Chap. III and Chap. VI. The Macmillan Company.

Sperry, Willard L., *Reality in Worship*, Chap. VIII. The Macmillan Company.

Vogt, Von Ogden, *Modern Worship*, Chap. IV. Yale University Press.

Vogt, Von Ogden, *Art and Religion*. Yale University Press.

Wieman, Henry Nelson, *Methods of Private Religious Living*, Chaps. I, II, and VI. The Macmillan Company.

CHAPTER III

MAKING GOD REAL

I am aware,
As I go commonly sweeping the stair,
Doing my part of the everyday care,
Human and simple my lot and my share—
I am aware of a passion that pours
Down the channels of fire through Infinity's doors;
　　Forces terrific, with melody shod,
　　Music that mates with the pulses of God.

　．　．　．　．　．　．　．　．　．

I am aware,
As I sit quietly here in my chair,
Sewing or reading or braiding my hair—
Human and simple my lot and my share—

　．　．　．　．　．　．　．　．　．

I am aware of the splendor that ties
All the things of the earth with the things of the skies;
　　Here in my body the heavenly heat,
　　Here in my flesh the melodious beat
　　Of the planets that circle Divinity's feet,
As I sit silently here in my chair,
　　I am aware."

　　　　　　　　　　　　　　—Angela Morgan.

From "Kinship," in *The Hour Has Struck*, pp. 19-20. Dodd,
Mead and Company. Used by permission.

A writer from the Orient, in a recent magazine
article, makes a plea for more first-hand religion in our
present-day living. Jesus' great contribution was a vital,
living companionship with his God. To-day, says this
writer, we spend our time calling attention to his life
and his religious experience instead of attempting to

experience for ourselves that same vital relationship with God.

Perhaps it is not so easy in a scientific age, with its emphasis upon cosmic energy as the power undergirding the universe, to think of God in terms of personality. And perhaps, with this uncertainty as to just how *personal* God is, it is difficult to maintain a sense of the reality of God. Yet even in days gone by, when the thought that man was created in his image gave God a distinctly human aspect, although God was definitely conceived as a real Personality, there was often lacking a reality of personal experience of this God. There is the possibility that by thinking of him as less local and human and as more pervading and spiritual, men may come to a greater vividness of experience and a sense of the reality of his presence.

Undoubtedly, there is much unreality of religious experience, and undoubtedly many lives could be released from fear, maladjustment, anxiety, friction, vagueness, and indifference to that more abundant life of constructive living, if God were somehow more real and if men were conscious of being fully at one with the purpose and power of God's life in the world. What we covet for our children and young people and adults is this consciousness that in God "we live and move and have our being," this awareness of God in the midst of all of life's experiences.

As we think about this, we realize that it may involve us in a consideration of the total program of religious education, for whether worship will be a real and desirable experience in the lives of our boys and girls will depend not entirely upon the character of the worship program itself, but also upon the kind of teaching they receive in their homes and in their church-school classes. If a child's response to God in a worship service is hindered because of some unwise home teaching or some unfortunate home condition, then it becomes an essential objective of the worship program to attempt to straighten out the home difficulty. All the worship-planning in the world will not help a little child to love and worship a Father God if his experience in his own home is with an unkind or inadequate father. And an adolescent will find it difficult to pray to a God of love in his young people's worship service if he has been brought up at home with a concept of a God who sends disaster upon innocent people.

So we can see that the program of adult education in the church may contribute very directly to the effectiveness of the worship program. Adult classes on "What Shall I Teach My Child?" or "What Shall I Think About Religion?" may become one of the essential items in a total program of worship for any church.

If the teacher in the church school in her own confused thinking uses the words "God" and "Jesus" interchangeably and so confuses a little child (as one teacher actually did) that he relates at home that "Jesus made the world; my teacher says so," then the program for the training of teachers is immediately involved. Teachers must be helped to clarify their own thinking before they can guide the thinking of others.

If boys and girls are being taught by teachers with unbalanced personalities, or if parents themselves need help in personality adjustment, then these personality difficulties of teachers and parents will need to be straightened out so as to make a happier, more normal religious experience possible for boys and girls. If, in matters of discipline in the church school, Mary feels that she is not understood, or Fred feels that his teacher is too autocratic, or a class of first-year junior high-school girls feels that their teacher is "not interested" in them or takes her church-school teaching lightly, the sense of injustice or the feeling of dislike for church school will surely set limits upon the ability of these young people to enter into a satisfying worship experience with their groups. It is at this point that the problem of the selection and supervision of teachers cuts across the problem of worship.

With this thought of the interrelatedness of the worship program with the total church program in mind, let us see if there are ways in which people can be helped so that God may seem real to them and they may know how to find him and to relate themselves to him in a vital way.

MAKING GOD REAL THROUGH HOME TRAINING

The child's first experience of God is related to his home and to his parents. Long before the earliest direct teaching about God can be given to him he can feel in the atmosphere about him the presence or absence of a divine reality.

Home Atmosphere. A sense of calm and quiet in the atmosphere about him, a feeling of poise and harmony in and among the adults of the household, the child senses in the very touch with which he is handled, in the tones of the voices about him, and in the expressions on the faces which later he comes to read for their every meaning. Some sense of calm and repose is needed for a genuine experience of God, and the child is less apt to have this experience in homes that are tense with the pressure of too many things to do or hectic with the rush of unorganized activities.

Value of Leisure. There is need too for leisure in the home for the enjoyment of the best things which life has to offer. There must be time in which home ideals can operate and the love of all that is finest can be developed. To look at beautiful pictures, to listen to beautiful music, to enjoy the great literature of the past and the present, and to share all of this enjoyment of beauty with the family group, is an experience which can serve as a background for an understanding of God.

Power of Suggestion. Not only is the home atmosphere important, but the power of suggestion is potent in making God real to the children and young people in the home. Is God real to the fathers and mothers as they go about their daily living? Does the child feel that his parents are calm in the presence of a crisis, happy in the face of trouble, buoyed up by their perfect adjustment to a Power that is greater than they?

Do the parents share the experiences of prayer with each other and with the children? And is the whole experience of family worship made so inviting that the children look forward to it as a privilege and not as a duty?

We must remember that the power of suggestion works only under certain conditions and by certain laws.[1] Charters says that the "suggester should possess the confidence of the subject." The one suggesting must feel and show enthusiasm for the attitude which he is suggesting. Parents who are chums and playmates with their children will have a larger chance of winning them

---

[1] See Charters, *The Teaching of Ideals,* Chap. XI, "Suggestion and Example."

to a desire to worship. If they share with their children in all of their experiences of play and school, it will be easier to share with them the greatest experience of all.

The Character of Home Discipline. The character of home discipline will affect the child's response to the religion of his parents. If the discipline is of the autocratic type, if there is constant suppression of normal childhood impulses, so that a barrier of feeling is built up between parents and children, then that same barrier will shut out any common experience of God. But in homes where difficulties are settled as little as possible by formal discipline but largely by an attempt at cooperative understanding, and where the children and young people feel that parents are, above everything else, in sympathy with them—in such homes there is the possibility that the children will be susceptible to the suggestion of parents.

As young people approach adolescence it is especially important that they shall feel admiration for their parents. If adolescents feel that their parents belong to an older generation, that they are one-sided personalities, lacking an interest in the wide range of experiences which are so thrilling to youth, and that they do not understand youth's point of view, then the religion of these same parents will appear only as the excessive piety of unbalanced personalities, instead of the natural expression of radiant lives. Yes, the suggester must seem as desirable as the experience which he wishes to suggest.

Parents often do not realize that there may be a close relationship between the child's religious concepts and the physical and psychological care which he receives. The child whose body early becomes a perfect working organism, subject to fine control, has a basis laid for an experience of God. He comes to *feel* first, and later *understand* law and order in the universe. Mrs. Fahs, in an article on "The Beginnings of Religion in Baby Behavior," says of the child who learns while he is a baby that he is the most beloved and most important person in the world, "If he were fully conscious of what he had done and could tell us, he might say something like this: 'The people and things around me exist especially for my benefit. I am king in this kingdom. I own the world.' . . . When parent or teacher present to him a picture of a loving Heavenly Father, it will be pleasant and easy for him to accept the thought of his being a favorite with God. The Santa Claus God will fit nicely into his life picture. When, however, disillusionment and disappointment necessarily come, there will probably be resentment, as was the case of one such boy who said, 'I hate God because he won't give me an electric train.' It will be natural for a 'mamma's baby,' who finds himself less capable in practical life than those of his own age, to grasp at the possibility of living close to God and of becoming like him. The God wish, instead of encouraging him to grow and achieve value, may become a way of retreating from the need to be efficient and useful. His feeling of power will come with his daydreaming and his praying."[2]

This description of one type of home training is given to show at how early an age religious concepts are being formed, and that the connection between the child's ability to enter into an enriching relationship with God through worship and his home training is in reality a very close one. It would be well if relationships of this

---

[2] From *Religious Education,* December, 1930, p. 899.

sort were pointed out and discussed in parents' meetings in the church.

Sincerity in Religious Experience of Parents. Young people in the home must feel that back of this God-experience which their parents wish to share with them there is the utmost sincerity. They will sooner or later detect the difference between gushing sentimentality in matters of religion and radiant conviction. One of the tests of this sincerity will be in the consistency of the lives which the adults live. "By their fruits ye shall know them," and children and young people are alert and sensitive to the "fruits" in daily living. To the power of suggestion must be joined the force of example. If God is to be real to childhood and youth, then adults in the home must speak and live as they teach and pray.

We cannot teach that God will help us overcome fear and then live our lives under the bondage of all sorts of fears. We cannot expect our children to believe that God is good and continually show evidences of being harassed by worry and anxiety. We cannot invite our boys and girls to turn to God for strength and poise while we are living examples of loss of self-control.

The Home and the Concept of God. What we sometimes fail to realize is that the very concept, itself, of God as a Father of a great spiritual family must be acquired from a Godlike home. This does not mean a home where observance of family prayers is enforced or where Sunday means "God's day" as separated from all the other days. It means, rather, a home where the parents are so perfectly mated physically, mentally and spiritually that there is possible a richness of common experience between husband and wife and so much of joy shining through it all that the children find it easy to feel that God is near.

Teaching in the Home. While home atmosphere is felt long before any teaching about God can be appreciated by the child, and while suggestion and example of parents are the most potent kind of teaching, yet the home has a supreme opportunity to offer direct teaching about God and prayer and worship to the children. Since the earliest impressions are apt to be so vivid and so lasting, sometimes children never rid themselves of the concepts formed through their early teachings.[3]

There is the opportunity too in the home for repeated emphasis, and as yet, under our present system, the time for religious education outside the home is very limited. One of the weaknesses of a great deal of our teaching in church-school classes is that so much of it is teaching without living. To some extent this cannot be avoided, since teacher and child cannot live through *many* experiences together. However, in the home what is taught may be lived and teaching about God may grow out of actual situations which reveal him or can be guided so as to open up new truths about him.

Worship in the Home. In making God real in the home, there is no substitute for the actual experience of worship, if parents conduct this family worship with an understanding of the needs and interests of their children and of the psychology which makes a rich worship experience possible.

If God is to seem real, family worship as well as worship planned for church-school groups should meet

---

[3] For a consideration of children's religious concepts, see Baker, *Worship of the Little Child*, Chap. III; Blashfield, *Worship Training for Primary Children*, Chaps. I and VIII; Jones, *Training Juniors in Worship*, Chap. II.

the real problems of child and adolescent life and of the family life together. If the children in a home are of near age, this will be easier. However, in the small family group it is easier to tie the divergent interests together than in larger school groups. There are stories and poems which are simple enough for the youngest, yet rich enough in content for the oldest to appreciate.

Family worship will have to be planned to meet the changing standards and customs of the American home. In the following case note the wisdom of the parents in fitting the worship experience into the time schedule of a suburban home and of introducing it at a natural time and in a natural way. Note also their consideration of the changing attitudes of their boys and their feeling that family worship is *family* worship, as personal and intimate as our individual private worship.

In a modern home in the suburb of a large city, where the father must commute several hours each day, the family decided upon the few minutes after the evening dinner for their family worship hour. There were four boys in the family ranging from high-school age down to first grade. During the dinner the father and mother gradually turned their thoughts to some big issues, so that the transition from fun (and there was plenty of it in this family) to the prayer period was not abrupt. After some informal conversation they bowed their heads and each one offered a prayer beginning with the parents and going down to the youngest.

The mother says that she has always watched for any signs that the boys were tiring of this hour and then introduced a new way of doing things. Perhaps it would be something to read; possibly something in current life similar to some Bible incident. Always the boys were taken into partnership and asked *how* they would like the hour conducted. Once they tired of praying themselves and wanted written prayers to read for a change. Visitors in the home were never admitted to this intimate glimpse of family life unless they were old, old friends whom the boys trusted and wanted to have share this experience of worship with them.

Even in the midst of our highly organized living to-day it is possible to find brief periods when families may share spiritual insight and enjoy together the things of the spirit. One family in the summer months often packs up the Sunday dinner after church and takes it out to the woods. There, after the noon meal, in the quiet and hush of the forest, some nature poetry is read aloud and there is time to listen to the silence. The Sunday-evening supper hour can be made a high spot in the week's activities, a time when all share the preparation of the meal, and when, before the open fire, special stories are read or books which stretch the soul out to wonder. One young minister kept one family in his parish supplied with a reading list of books appropriate for their Sunday-evening hour together. The church, through its leadership, ought to be of greater service to homes which want help in planning home worship.

Home and Church Working Together. To make companionship with God the richest possible experience for our boys and girls, there should be the closest co-operation between the home and the church or any other agencies which are determining the religious education of the child.

Since the child's relationship to God is the most fundamental experience of his whole life, parents ought to be greatly concerned to know all about the program of worship in which he participates in the church. Parents ought to be interested to know what their children are being taught in the church school.

If the church attempts to cultivate the worship life of the child through an adequate program, and the child worships God in his church, while his home is indifferent and does not encourage the "practice of the presence of God," the child will begin to feel that religion and the actual business of living are entirely unrelated. In this way there develops an unreality of religious experience. If, on the other hand, the home encourages a vital worship experience which is far more satisfying than anything offered by the church, the young person will approach his church with a critical attitude or he will not approach it at all, finding its spiritual offering too meager to satisfy his demands for a full, rich life.

If worship is to flower into Godlike character in everyday living, the home and the church must work together to this end, for it is in the home that the little child finds his greatest opportunity, and older children one of their chief opportunities of living out the ideals stimulated by worship. When ideals do not become operative in life, when they allure with their beauty in moments of reflective enjoyment, but remain merely objects of admiration without becoming controlling factors in conduct, there may arise a duality in consciousness, which fosters unreality in the religious experience.

The Worship Needs of Adults. There is nothing which will make adults so conscious of the worship needs of the youth of the church as participation themselves Sunday after Sunday in enriching worship experiences.

In a church where the minister feels that adults in the modern world need more than anything else a sense of fellowship with God through worship, and where adults find this need of theirs met every Sunday through satisfying worship services and fill the pews long before the hour for church to begin, we are not surprised to learn that in this church the adults have a real concern for the worship needs of the children and young people. The minister himself is personally interested in and helps to plan the worship program for the children, beginning with those of nursery-school age. But he does not stop with the boys and girls. He carries his program of education for worship on through the adult years in the attempt to help the adult church members understand why they need to worship and why worship takes the form which it does in their church. Parents in this church, talking with strangers after the morning service, will almost invariably explain about the church's worship program for boys and girls, for the adults in this church have become worship-conscious.

However, it is not only because they are leaders of youth that adults need to have their worship needs met. Every adult has a life of his own to live. Because he is a parent or a teacher he need not submerge his own personality. On the other hand, he will be a more effective parent or teacher in so far as he leads a rich, full life himself. Jesus surely had adults as well as youth in mind when he said, "I am come that they might have life, and might have it abundantly." As surely as he said, "Suffer the little children to come," he talked with a woman by a well, and he unfolded the secret of a happy life to Zacchæus. Yes, Jesus, with all his reverence for the unfolding personality of a little child, had the most infinite respect for the personality of the adult. It was to great crowds of eager, listening adults that he told those incomparable stories of the life that is more than raiment, and it was of such a multitude of adults that the old record says that he "was moved with compassion toward them, because they were as sheep not having a shepherd: and he began to teach them many things."

MAKING GOD REAL THROUGH OUR TEACHING

We have seen what an important part early teaching plays in the child's religious experience. His earliest concepts of God and his early formed attitudes toward the religious life will do much either to inhibit or make possible a satisfying experience of communion with God. The adults in the church, then, including the minister, parents, and teachers, are vitally concerned about the ideas which the youth of the church are acquiring through the church's program of religious education.

Adequate Concepts. We can help the child by giving him no ideas which he will have to unlearn later on. This is not an easy thing to do. "What is God like?" asks the child. Can we answer him so that he will think of God as all-good and all-love, and yet not make the picture of him so definite and so final that there is no room left for the child himself to form his own conception and to embark upon the adventure of exploring, through first-hand experience, the character of God?

It is not always possible to avoid the "unlearning" process. All of us, if we grow at all, are constantly discarding old ideas, as we learn newer and truer ones. But if we teach boys and girls not with dogmatism, but constantly emphasizing the fact that men are continually making discoveries about God and that life holds some mysteries beyond the farthest thought of man, we may prepare our young people to learn new truths without becoming emotionally upset.

There are at least three avenues through which the pupils in our church schools acquire their ideas of God: through the teaching in their classes, through the concepts of God contained in the textbooks of religious education, and through the worship services themselves.

Doctor McLean, in his investigation of the ideas of God held by Protestant children, lists the following terms by which God was addressed in a number of worship services:

Father, Heavenly Father, Jehovah, Father, Son, and Holy Ghost; Lord of Heaven and Earth and Sea, Lord God Almighty, Lord of Hosts, Father of All, Almighty Father, King Eternal, Almighty King, The Most High God, God of Love, Creator, King of Love, Shepherd, God of Glory, The God of My Salvation, Friend, Loving Father, Everlasting Father.

It is not to be wondered at that children are confused in their thinking about God, nor that adolescents and adults find themselves burdened with concepts which hinder rather than encourage satisfying worship experiences.

Doctor Betts has pointed out the wide differences of opinion which exist among theologians and ministers as to what we shall teach about God.[4] And if theologians and ministers do not agree, we cannot expect that laymen will do so either. In fact, we do not want to insist that all shall think about God in just the same way. Nor is it desirable that anyone's thinking about God shall be final. Room must be left for growth and

---

[4] George Herbert Betts, *Teaching Religion To-day*, Chap. VIII, "God in Our Teaching." The Abingdon Press.

development in our thinking about God as in all our thinking and living.

The leader of worship should select all worship materials not only for their appropriateness to the theme and their suitability for the age group, but also for the helpfulness of the religious concepts found in them.

Let us, in all our worship planning, remember how important in an individual's religious experience is his concept of God and his consequent attitude toward God. As leaders of childhood and youth we have a share, through our teaching and through our living, in painting the picture of God for them. The following poem suggests how some of the artists have painted him:

"I wonder sometimes at their idea of God,
  These great artists who painted for the Catholic Kings.
  He is an old man, their God; senile, white-fringed man, decaying visibly.
  Raphael has a little flying God Almighty on the sky, carrying two unborn babies in his arms.
  A little busy body, white-haired God, powerful as a moth, he paints him.
  Tintoretto's puny God looks worried, though poised in Paradise at the top of things, above Jesus and Mary and the adoring circle of saints—
How could they adore that God?
How would you paint God?
God, eternally young, young as the sun,
  Young as Orion's nebula.
God the creator, stringing worlds like pearls in the sky.
God, molding our earth after supper of the day he had spread the milky way like a carpet for his feet,
  Fingering forth men in millions with his right hand, and beasts, birds, fishes with his left.
God, smiling at life as at a field of nodding flowers,
God, fecund, magnificent, glorious.
God, of the love intonable, love dark and bright, that searches, challenges, rewards.
God, moving forever at the center, with space like a thin robe around him,

God, facing his universe ever beginning and ending and calling it a day.

God of the blazing eyes that see,
God of the secret ears that hear,
God of Light, Light of Light, very God of our God,
How would you paint God?"[5]

So important is this matter of acquiring adequate
religious concepts that it may be well to point out in a
general way how inadequate are some ideas, as well as
to suggest a few fundamental concepts which will make
communion with God possible.

Some adolescents have confessed that though intellectually they know that God is a Spirit, still when they
close their eyes to pray, they are often bothered by
graphic pictures of an old man, a throne, a very pic-
torial scene of a Father, Son, and Holy Spirit around
a throne, or other distracting images. So vivid is this
imagery that it often requires an act of will to get rid
of it. In this way some of the energy of the spirit
which might be released for prayer goes into the effort
to reconstruct the ideas before real prayer can take place.

Other inadequate concepts have included God the
All-Seeing Eye, God the Judge and punisher, God the
Magic Worker who performs miracles, or who can be
wheedled into granting our requests. Often God has
become localized on a throne, or "up" somewhere above
the clouds.

In a brief text like this which must cover the entire
field of worship, it is not possible to discuss in detail
what we shall teach about God. But it may be well to

[5] Harriet Monroe, in *Poetry: A Magazine of Verse*, March, 1924.
Used by permission of author.

point out that concepts like the following will furnish a soil of thinking and feeling out of which a rich worship experience can grow.

1. *God is a friendly, loving God.* We must, at the outset, assume a belief in either a friendly or an unfriendly universe. Not only does human experience lead us to believe that God expresses himself through love, but to-day we have sufficient corroboration from scientists to say with confidence, "I believe in a friendly world and in a friendly God whose heart is love."

2. *God is law-abiding God.* The more we know about the cosmic processes that govern our universe, the more convinced we become that the world in which we live is built on an orderly design, and that it operates in accordance with law. We must believe that God himself does not break laws, but that he himself abides by, and works through the laws which he has established.

3. *God is an active, creative God.* Man can only worship satisfactorily a God who is creatively active now, who has not set his world going and then left it to spin along its way. The mind of man has discovered that the evolutionary process is going on to-day as it was in the beginning. In one of his poems, Louis Untermeyer tells us what Dick, aged six, says about heaven and God. In the closing lines Dick says:

> "But God just sits and never works at all,
>   And that's because he's God!"[6]

This is one type of an inadequate concept which will keep men from entering into a vital, active relationship with an actively creative God. Leaders of youth need to keep in touch with the current scientific thinking of

[6] From "Dick Said," in *This Singing World*, p. 210, Harcourt, Brace and Company, Inc.

the times so that God may be interpreted in terms of the newest discoveries of science and no possible revelation of his activity missed. A God who is still active in the universe and who is identified with the whole process of creation and the development of life is a more real God than one whose creative activity has ceased.

4. *God is an intelligent God.* All of the previous concepts imply a God who is intelligence—a Mind back of the universe, not blind chance. Ames says that God must be the expression of the three values found in all reality—love, order, and intelligence. We need not argue with questioning youth about the omniscience of God. Nor do we mean, when we say that God is Intelligence, that God uses his mind to count off our little deeds. But, we can turn the attention of youth to a God who makes intelligent plans, a God of whom we can say with Tennyson:

> "That God, which ever lives and loves,
>   One God, one law, one element,
>   And one far-off divine event,
> To which the whole creation moves."

5. *God is a powerful God.* Men seek in worship a God who has real power and sources of strength upon which they can draw. In the last analysis, the power which they seek is not that of an autocrat who moves men about as pawns or who deliberately sets aside the laws of a world which he has built upon law. The God whom men worship must be a God upon whom they can confidently depend because he has that power which comes through inherent goodness, perfect love, the pursuit of worthy goals, utterly sacrificial devotion, and an unshakable belief that mankind can become like him.

6. *God expresses himself through personality.* When

we say that the God whom man can worship satisfactorily expresses himself through personality, we do not mean that God is to be thought of as "a person." We need not so limit him; God may have other attributes in his relationship to the great universe of which we are a part. He may be that great creative energy which keeps the universe going and in his relationships with different parts of the cosmos he may express himself in other ways than through personality.

But, personality also may be one of his attributes. In addition to his cosmic relationships, he has relationships with human personalities, and personality must be the way in which he finds it possible to reveal himself to men and to enter into satisfactory communion with them.

7. *God is mystery.* Last of all, in our effort to answer the question, "What is God like?" we must acknowledge that there is a sense in which that question can never be completely answered. For the eternal God, though he is knowable, is at the same time unknowable. Men have always wondered what God is like, and men will go on crying out with the poet,

> "And everywhere
> That a thought may dare
>   To gallop, mine has trod—
> Only to stand
> At last on the strand
>   Where just beyond lies God."[7]

It is not within the scope of this book to suggest how these concepts of God shall be interpreted to growing personalities at each stage of their development. For such detailed treatment the reader must turn to books

---

[7] "The Mystic," by Cale Young Rice. Used by permission of author.

which deal with the needs of specific age groups. But we must remind ourselves that in early childhood the foundations are laid in our teaching for either helpful or non-helpful concepts of God, and that many adults in our churches need to have their thinking about God clarified. Every teacher needs to ask himself the searching question, "How would you paint God?"

It is not only necessary to see that children and adults have adequate concepts of God, but also that their thinking is not confused. Confused thinking means that some of the energy which ought to be released for co-operative union with the purposes of God through worship is consumed in trying to find a way out of the confusion. There are some forms of confusion which can be avoided under wise teaching.

Often the little child is confused about the relationship between God and Jesus: God is Jesus' Father; God is *our* Father, yet he hears prayers offered to Jesus. In our hymns we speak to God and then to Jesus, as though he were identical with God, sometimes in the same hymn. This inaccuracy of thinking makes God less real. The child should be taught to offer his prayers to God, and not to Jesus. The simple, straightforward story of the beautiful life of Jesus should suggest to him that he too is God's child just as Jesus was, and that he too may enjoy that wonderful companionship with God which made Jesus' life so radiant.

Sincerity in Worship. Absolute sincerity in one's religious experience is necessary if God is to be a real factor. In the Corcoran Art Gallery in Washington there stands a statue of a four-year-old, with hands pressed together in the attitude of prayer. But down the little child's cheeks great tears are rolling, and one does not need to look at the inscription in the marble below to know that this is "Forced Prayer." The desire to pray should be stimulated before the child is asked to pray. Prayer should come as the result of a felt need or a real desire. Otherwise we fall into the habit of praying with the lips what we do not really mean and there results an unreality of religious experience.

In services of worship prayers which are too long and outlast the span of the worshiper's attention often have this same regrettable result—the unreality of the worship experience.

The saying of hymns, prayers, creeds which we do not understand will have the same effect. All such materials of worship need to be studied for their meaning and their significance for the worshiping group,[8] so that they may be a real expression of individual belief. Hymns or creeds which the worshiper does not believe will often make the whole experience of worship unreal.

The Method of Teaching. The method of teaching as well as its content will influence the reality of the God experience. In order that ideas may be clear and accurate, that perplexities may be straightened out and thinking crystallized, there should be free and frequent conversation with children and group discussion with adolescents and adults. This is particularly necessary if groups are to meet on a common ground of understanding of the purposes of their worship together.

We need to help the individual develop a technique of worship and prayer. Streeter calls this "the language of worship." Many do not enter into the full possibilities of private or public worship because they do not know what to do or how to go about it. Children, young

---

[8] See Chap. X, "Preparation for Worship."

people, and adults all need suggestions as to some effective methods of private worship.[9]

The whole teaching process can vitally affect the pupil's worship experience. If the teaching and curriculum are of such a nature that God is associated with life's everyday situations, then we may expect our youth to feel with the poet:

"I am aware of the splendor that ties
All the things of the earth with the things of the skies."

Experiences of Working With God. One of the best ways in which to make God real is to provide through the church program, for old and young, opportunities of working with God in activities which will make the world better. People will come to a realization of what God is like by sharing in God's processes of creative activity. Kirby Page makes this suggestion to adults living in this modern age, when he links with the necessity for silence and meditation the important work of relieving human misery and the establishment of social justice.[10]

But no child is too young to feel that he and God are partners in making the world a better place for all people to live in. The following litany could only have been written by a group of children who had first of all lived through the experiences which the litany describes. By entering into experiences of understanding and helpfulness their knowledge of God was not confined to intellectual concepts, though these were present, but was that knowledge which comes through the sharing of a common purpose.

[9] See *Methods of Private Religious Living*, by Henry N. Wieman. The Macmillan Company, New York.
[10] See *Living Creatively*, by Kirby Page. Farrar and Rinehart.

MAKING GOD REAL

A Litany of Thanks for God's Love Working in People

Dear God, we are studying about your world, and as we study, we keep finding you at work in it.

Where people are crowded together in the city we find men like Jacob Riis, trying to make things better. We find women like Jane Addams, trying to make people happier. For these men and women,

ALL: We thank you, God.

Where great ships land, bringing people from other countries, we find friendly teachers who try to make the first days here pleasant. Where guests from far away might be lonely, we find places where they may live together and make friends. For teachers at Ellis Island, and for International House,

ALL: We thank you, God.

Where people are homesick for books which they can understand and read, we find libraries with shelves and shelves of books written in many languages, we find rooms where even the blind may read. For the friendly thoughts which built our library,

ALL: We thank you, God.

Where children need love and care, we find homes like the Sheltering Arms. For the helpers in these homes,

ALL: We thank you, God.

For policemen who care for the helpless, for doctors and nurses who care for the sick, for all those who are working with you to make a safer, happier world,

ALL: We thank you, God.

And now may your spirit be with us, O God. We know there is much yet to do. Help us to remember that you are depending on us to make this world still better. Amen.[11]

Making God Real Through the Worship Program of the Church

One of the very important functions of the worship program in the church is to make God seem real and near. Those who plan the curriculum of worship must keep this aim before them constantly. There are some

[11] From *As Children Worship*, by Jeannette E. Perkins. Copyright, The Pilgrim Press. Used by permission.

77

forms which worship may take which may give the experience a greater tone of reality than others.

In a progressive day school a group of fourth-grade children were taken to another room to see an exhibit of curios from India. Among other objects was a carved wooden snake which the woman in charge of the exhibit said was worshiped by the people in that part of India. On the way back to their own room the children were talking with each other earnestly. Since this was a school of the freer type, they were allowed to walk along in informal groups, talking to each other. When they came back to their own room they gathered in a group, still talking earnestly. The teacher listened and let them talk. They apparently had forgotten they had a teacher. The conversation was somewhat as follows:

Richard: I think that's foolishness. Praying to a snake.

Helen: Why, Richard White, it isn't a bit foolish. You've got to pray to something, and if you don't know anything better than a snake, it's all right.

Richard: No 'taint. It's foolish for anybody to pray to a snake.

Mary: Well, I don't think it's so foolish.

Richard: Well, it is. It's dumb. It's foolish to pray at all. How do we know there's any God? (*Cries of shocked protest from most of the children.*)

Helen: Why, of course there's a God, Richard White. Don't you know God made you?

Richard: Shucks! He didn't either. I know how I was made.

John: But, there is a God.

Richard: How do you know? You can't see him.

Helen: Well, there are lots of things you can't see, but they're real, just the same.

Richard: What?

Helen: Well, there's electricity.

Richard: Pooh! I can see electricity. There it is, right there. (*Pointing to the electric-light bulb.*)

Helen: You don't see the electricity. You see a light. So, you know electricity is there. But, you can't see the electricity.

Richard (still unconvinced): Well, I don't care. I don't believe there's a God.

(*At this point some of the children appeared to remember the teacher for the first time, and one of them spoke.*)

Ruth: Miss R., what do you think? Don't you believe there is a God?

Miss R. (who up to this moment had been pretending to be busy with some books, but who had been listening eagerly): "Yes, I believe there is a God. This morning as I came to school I saw the lilacs beginning to show their purple heads on the bushes, and the tulips in the gardens along the way, and I thought how only a few weeks ago there were no flowers in the gardens, yet every spring they come again to make the world beautiful. And I thought of the wonderful Mind that planned how things should grow. Then, I looked up into the blue sky and saw the little white, floating clouds blowing across the blue, and I remembered the rain that came night before last to make the buds come out and the sun that is shining so bright and warm to-day, and again I thought of Someone who planned the rains and the sunshine. I saw all the boys and girls running into school, and I thought of all their happy homes and how Somebody has planned that we shall not live alone, but has set us in homes with fathers and mothers and brothers and sisters, so we are not lonely. And I said to myself: 'Isn't it a wonderful world? Who puts the kind thoughts into our minds and makes us want to help our mothers and be kind to people and who made us so that we think of all the happy, helpful things to do for each other?' "

The teacher paused for a moment, and in the silence Richard gave a little sigh, the tense look about his mouth and eyes relaxed, and he spoke as though a great burden had rolled off his shoulders: "So, that is what you call God!"[12]

An Active and Informal Program. An active as over against a stilted program for our boys and girls sometimes is the means of placing them in situations which will naturally reveal to the group the need of worship or which will arouse a desire for it. If the group is

---

[12] Reprinted from *Junior Method in the Church School*, by Marie Cole Powell, pp. 378-380. The Abingdon Press, New York. Used by permission.

engaged in some common enterprise, there may come moments when worship grows out of the real experience of the group. It is at such times as these that God seems very real to the pupil and the classroom or department room becomes a piece of life itself.

Let us suppose that the group of children described above had been a church-school group instead of a day-school group. After the discussion had culminated in Richard's sigh of relief, "So, that is what you call God !" it would have been the most natural thing in the world for the leader to have said, "Do you want to speak to God for a minute and tell him how glad we are that he finds so many ways of speaking to us ?"

Worship Growing Out of Actual Situations. This is what we mean when we talk of worship growing out of the experience of pupils. In the process of seeking solutions for problems we often discover that we need God's help. In the sudden realization of happiness, we often want to pause and thank God for it. When we suddenly discern a new truth or catch a vision of something fine and noble, there is an outreach of our personality toward God.

Often these experiences of insight or illumination occur in actual life. Therefore, if we want our boys and girls to learn to seek this type of companionship with God in the midst of life's experiences, we must make the classroom a piece of life itself. Active processes must be going on. In the place of passive sitting, we must encourage active participation. Instead of presenting problems of thinking to our pupils, we must more and more seek to place our groups in situations where they will feel their own problems and try to find a solution.

A Flexible Program. The implications of all this, as

far as method is concerned, are far-reaching. It means a more flexible program. For one contributing element to the reality of such worship experiences will be the fact that opportunity for worship is given at the moment when the group is ready for it.

Worship by Grades. Another implication *may be* worship by grades rather than by departments. For worship can only occur in such a natural way when all the group is engaged in the same task. When we are all working on the same enterprise, when we are attacking the same problem, and when worship grows out of the needs revealed to us as we think and work together, we have an integration of the entire morning's activity, which suggests how life itself ought to be lived.

The Opportunity for the Class Teacher. The class teacher has a supreme opportunity to guide his group into situations where worship moments of this spontaneous and informal character naturally occur. If the department is large and if three grades worship together in a more formal type of worship experience, the class teacher may feel that he has an enviable opportunity to enter into worship experiences of this more spontaneous type with his group. Many a class period may culminate in a moment of worship. Frequently we may worship in the midst of a class session. Happy is that teacher who realizes that he too, as well as the department superintendent, may kindle the torch of worship in the life of youth!

In actual life when we are caught by the spell of a mountain sunset, and feelings akin to worship begin to surge up within us, we do not cut the experience short and say, "Not now; but later, when I get back home, I will appreciate this and thank God for it." We *may* later on, through the power of recollection, recall our pleasure in the sunset and offer our gratitude for the privilege of such enjoyment, but there is a certain reality in the immediate experience in the presence of the sunset which brings God very near.

There is a place in life for both types of worship, that which is "celebration of life,"[13] and that which is life in the living. If we want boys and girls and young people, and, later on, adults, to have this awareness of God not only in moments of planned worship but in the midst of life itself, we shall have to plan, at least occasionally, to let worship occur in the church school at such places and such times as it naturally arises. It is not only

"In temples and cathedrals dim,
Through vigil, chant, and prayer,"

that we want our youth to feel God near. But also we want them to know in practice as well as theory that

"Wherever man cries out to God,
The living God is there."

ADDITIONAL READING SOURCES

General

Hocking, W. E., *The Meaning of God in Human Experience*. Yale University Press.

International Council of Religious Education, *Curriculum Guide*, Books I, II, and III.

Strickland, Francis L., *The Psychology of Religious Experience*. Abingdon Press.

Suter, John W., Jr., *Open Doors in Religious Education*. Chap. I, "Toward Deeper Knowledge"; Chap. II, "Toward Better Worship." Harper & Brothers.

Van Deusen, Henry Pitt, *The Plain Man Seeks for God*. Charles Scribner's Sons.

Religious Ideas

American Institute of Sacred Literature, University of Chicago

[13] See Von Ogden Vogt, *Modern Worship*, Chap. I.

Press. *Finding God Through the Beautiful. Experiments in Personal Religion.*

Harkness, Georgia, *Conflicts in Religious Thought*. Henry Holt & Co.

Mather, Kirtley F., *Science in Search of God*. Henry Holt & Co.

McLean, Angus, *Ideas of God in Protestant Religious Education*. Columbia University Press.

Gilkey, James Gordon, *Meeting the Challenge of Modern Doubt*. The Macmillan Company.

Newton, Joseph Fort, *My Idea of God*. Little, Brown & Co.

Streibert, Muriel, *Youth and the Bible*. The Macmillan Company.

Strong, Sidney, *How to Find God*. Association Press.

Tittle, Ernest F., *The Religion of the Spirit*. The Abingdon Press.

Kirkland, Winifred, *Portrait of a Carpenter*. Charles Scribner's Sons.

Mental Hygiene and the Experience of Worship

Gilkey, James Gordon, *Managing One's Self*.

Groves, E. R., and Blanchard, Glydis H., *Wholesome Marriage*. Houghton Mifflin Company.

Lichliter, McIlyar H., *The Healing of Souls*. The Methodist Book Concern.

Overstreet, Harry, *About Ourselves*. W. W. Norton & Co.

Oliver, John Rathbone, *Psychiatry and Mental Health*. Charles Scribner's Sons.

Weatherhead, Leslie, *Psychology in the Service of the Soul*. The Macmillan Company.

Worship Experience for Children

Baker, Edna Dean, *The Worship of the Little Child*. The Methodist Book Concern.

Blashfield, Clara Beers, *Worship Training for Primary Children*. The Methodist Book Concern.

Fox, H. W., *The Child's Approach to Religion*. Harper & Brothers.

Hartshorne, Hugh, *Childhood and Character*. The Pilgrim Press.

Jones, Mary Alice, *Training Juniors in Worship*. Cokesbury Press.

Mother, by a, *The Problems of a Little Child*. The Pilgrim Press.

GUIDING THE EXPERIENCE OF WORSHIP

Mumford, Edith E. Read, *The Dawn of Religion in the Mind of the Child*. Longmans, Green & Co.

Perkins, Jeannette, *As Children Worship*. The Pilgrim Press.

Perkins, Jeannette, *Others Call It God*. Harper & Brothers.

Sweet, Helen F., and Fahs, Sophia L., *Exploring Religion With Eight Year Olds*. Henry Holt & Co.

Worship Experience for Young People

Brooks, Fowler D., *The Psychology of Adolescence*. Houghton Mifflin Company.

Jones, Rufus, *Finding the Trail of Life*. The Macmillan Company.

Sadler, William, *Piloting Modern Youth*. Funk & Wagnalls Company.

Shaver, E. L., and Stock, H. T., *Training Young People in Worship*. The Pilgrim Press.

CHAPTER IV

PLANNING THE WORSHIP PROGRAM OF THE CHURCH

In the large sense of the word, therefore, the ordering and conduct of public worship is the distinctive task of the church, and so long as this office is by common consent delegated to the church, the church need not complain that it is an outworn and superfluous institution. In seeming to do nothing for the world, it does all for the world, or at least that without which no human effort can ever be made perfect. . . .

So long as the church bids men to the worship of God and provides a simple and credible vehicle for worship it need not question its place, mission, and influence in the world.—W. L. SPERRY.

    In *Reality in Worship*, p. 168, The Macmillan Company.

HAPPY is that church which can speak in terms of the *church's* program of worship. To think in terms of a *church* program implies that the worship needs of the entire membership, from the youngest child in the home and in the nursery school to the oldest adult, are being provided for intelligently and are part of a comprehensive plan for growth and guided development in the experience of worship. This is the ideal which each church should set up for itself.

Such a comprehensive goal includes all the opportunities for worship which the church offers to its members. This means the Sunday worship services, morning, evening, or vesper; the worship services in the church school; all the worship experiences participated in at young people's meetings, missionary societies, midweek activities, and clubs for all ages; as well as worship in the home, either family worship or personal devotions.

The minister as guide. The minister who has such a comprehensive ideal for the worship program of the local church will not be able personally to plan or supervise all these worship experiences in detail, but he will be interested to know that all these needs are being cared for and that leaders of worship are being developed who can skillfully guide the worship experiences of each age group. The pastor of the small church often will have to assume more leadership than if the church were larger and had more lay leadership available.

At least once or twice a year the pastor might meet with all who are in any way responsible for the worship program of the groups within the church to share with them his knowledge of the nature and purpose of worship, leaving group leaders to make detailed plans. He will be most successful in his leadership in this field if he has a broad and sympathetic understanding of the worship needs of children, youth, and adults, and if he recognizes that the type of worship expression must vary for different age groups. That pastor will achieve the richest results who does not have any one set pattern of worship which he thinks must be adopted for all ages, but who trusts the leadership of those who have been trained to work with specific age groups and who rejoices when they are capable of planning for the worship needs of their own departments with initiative and creative enthusiasm.

The Sunday Worship Service. One of the worship objectives of the church is that every member may eventually seek and find spiritual enrichment through the worship experience provided at its Sunday-morning service. Any church ought to keep this objective in mind in planning its program.

We have already seen in previous chapters the necessity for graded worship,[1] if real life needs are to be met and if worship is to be a vital experience for all ages. We have also seen some of the possibilities inherent in the occasional sharing of corporate worship by old and young.[2] The different departments of the church school and affiliated groups are designed to care for these graded worship needs. But, one of their objectives should be to plan so that pupils in the church school also feel that they share the corporate worship experience of the church as a whole.

Different churches have sought this objective in different ways. Some of the most common methods are by having children remain for a part of the adult Sunday service, by devoting five minutes of the adult service to a children's sermon preached by the minister, by awards given to boys and girls who attend the adult services regularly, and by the organization of junior churches modeled in detail after the adult church organization and procedure. None of these methods seem really to accomplish the objective, which is to help children and young people to feel themselves a real part of the total church life and to provide a common experience of worship for old and young. Without listing the disadvantages of any of these methods, each of which probably has some values, perhaps the following constructive suggestions as to meeting this problem may stimulate churches to experiment with more fruitful methods:

[1] See Chap. II.
[2] See Chap. II.

1. When old and young worship together, plan worship experiences which grow out of interests which they have in common.

2. Select worship materials which are not too young for the adults but which the younger ones can appreciate, either because of their innate simplicity or because they have been first interpreted to them.

3. Fewer experiences of corporate worship planned in this way will do more to bind the young to the church than frequent attendance with adults upon services which have not been planned with the needs and interests of youth in mind.

4. A truly "shared experience of worship" must have its roots in a sharing of the total church enterprise. Old and young must actually *work* together if they are truly to *worship* together.

5. A minister can come to know the boys and girls of the church better and cement his relationship with them more strongly by meeting them in smaller groups when he may conduct worship *for them,* than by interrupting the continuity of the adult service of worship to preach a children's sermon.

6. It is most desirable that all age groups should worship occasionally in the church sanctuary. Departments of the church school can plan to have their worship services there several times a year. On occasion the minister may meet them and worship with them.

As boys and girls reach the adolescent years they are more ready to participate in the adult services of worship. They still have needs which are peculiarly their own and which should find expression and satisfaction in their own worship services in the church school and the young people's society. But, they should be helped to bridge the gap which so often exists between the young people's groupings and the church itself. Of course this gap should never exist, for, when young people enter into full church membership, some definite place should be made for them in the life of the church.

Some churches have attempted to solve this problem by having adolescents meet in the church school for their class work and then attend the morning worship, instead of having a worship service of their own. Undoubtedly, this is a better plan than for young people to participate in departmental worship services, where the leadership is inadequate and the services do not interest them. But it is as true of the church service as it is of their own departmental worship, that adolescents will attend if it meets the interests and needs of youth. Other churches have provided departmental worship to meet the peculiarly challenging problems of youth and have found ways of making the church worship so interesting and vital that young people have found it the most natural thing in the world to desire to attend that also. Many churches now have one Sunday each year when the young people of the church plan and conduct the morning worship.

Planning Departmental Programs of Worship

Let us now see what are the important steps in planning the worship program for a specific department. Let us remember that the suggestions made here are applicable, with modifications, to church-school departments or to any other groups which aim to minister to the worship life of individuals.

When we think of "planning the worship program" of the church, let us think more and more in terms of a democratic procedure. We are learning the educational value of plans which are initiated by pupils and teachers. We are coming to see that the best type of learning is real experiencing which is shared by leader, teachers, and pupils. We know that even little children can become conscious of the purposes of their own worship experiences, and can, under guidance, appraise some of the outcomes. A group of Primary children, planning with their leaders a worship service to help the incoming first grade feel at home and to help these newcomers to understand the worship service, made, among other suggestions, the following:

"We'll make them think of God by showing them the window because it makes us think that we should be friendly."

"We'll tell why we have old thoughts and new thoughts here."[3]

Knowing the Group Situation. As the first step in worship planning the leader or committee in charge of the worship program of any group must discover what are its real interests, problems, and needs. Some of these needs and interests are determined by the age of the members in the group, some by home, school or community situations. To plan worship adequately for any group a leader or committee must have an intimate understanding of the group situation and must know what are the interests and problems which are of concern to individuals in the group as well as to the group as a whole.

Determining Objectives for Worship. The next step is to determine how the worship services may be built

---

[3] From *As Children Worship*, by Jeannette E. Perkins. Copyright, The Pilgrim Press. Used by permission.

around these needs. This means that there must be clear-cut objectives for each worship service and materials discovered which will best interpret these objectives to the group and secure the desired outcomes in attitude and conduct. Let us imagine that the worship committee in a young people's department feels that a very special need of the group is to be assured of the reality of God in present experience. This need, then, becomes the worship objective for a series of worship services. To realize this objective the committee plans a series on the theme, "How God Speaks to Us." In order to lift the theme from vague generality, they plan a definite emphasis for successive Sundays, as, "God Speaks to Us Through Science," "God Speaks to Us Through Music," "God Speaks to Us Through Art," and "God Speaks to Us Through People."

Some have objected to the use of the word "theme" in that there may be danger of building worship services around themes instead of aiming to meet the needs of worshipers. We can avoid this if in our planning we always think first of the need to be met and write out clearly the definite objectives which we have in mind. As an example, the objectives of the service on the theme, "God Speaks to Us Through Science," might be:

To stimulate a worship experience (*a*) by using the discoveries of modern science as a revelation of God's continuous creativity. (*b*) By utilizing the personal testimonies of scientists to the conviction that God is "working his purpose out."

Planning for Various Types of Worship Experiences. When we think of the different forms which the experience of worship may take (those which were suggested in Chapter I), and when we recall the results in an individual's life which may accrue from a genuine worship experience, we realize that one important aspect of our planning is to provide services of worship which will cover all these needs. It is easy for a leader or a committee to become so interested in devising services of appreciation that they may forget the needed emphasis upon worship services with an ethical implication. On the other hand it sometimes happens that we become so engrossed with the need of solving problems that we overlook the fact that all of life is not problem-solving and that one of the important aspects of worship is the opportunity it affords the worshiper to express appreciation. Some services of worship must sound the note of challenge while others will aim to induce a mood of reassurance and of peace.

SELECTING THEMES FOR WORSHIP

We have already seen that the selection of a theme for a worship service is not the arbitrary choice of a subject but, rather, develops out of a study of group needs and is the attempt to build services that will have a clear-cut emphasis. The emphasis for each service is centered in some definite expression of the worshiper's relationship to God. On what basis, then, shall a leader or a committee go to work to select themes or define objectives for worship services?

To Meet Specific Needs. There are times when the themes for a series of worship services are suggested by some individual or group situation which reveals the fact that a certain type of worship experience is needed. Let us look at a few such situations and see how they might lead to the selection of worship objectives.

Harriet is in her third year of college. Her group of

friends is involved in an absorbed discussion about prayer. Let Harriet describe the situation: "One of our professors says that he doesn't believe any more that our prayers for another person can accomplish anything, especially if the other person doesn't know we are praying for him. Our crowd keeps discussing this. Now that I've begun to think about it, I can't pray any more until I find a satisfactory answer. My own worship life has just stopped. Every time I start to pray, something happens and I can't go on."

Here is a life situation which the worship program on the college campus ought to meet. Here is an opportunity for worship building for the college church, the college chapel, or the Sunday-evening young people's group to which Harriet's crowd belongs, or for several of these agencies working together.

Let us take as an illustration the fourth-grade group described in Chapter III.[4] The questioning about God, which started as a purely personal problem of Richard's, became a group problem as soon as the rest of the children commenced to think about it and to discuss it with such vehemence. Richard's declaration that there was no God suddenly broadened the thought horizons of his whole group, until the need for thoughtful conviction became a shared group experience. The problem for the church-school leader in such a situation would be so to plan the worship program for that group for the weeks immediately following that Richard would be helped to discover new evidence of God's reality, and that the whole group should have the beginning of a faith based, not merely on the experiences of others, but on their own experience of God as well.

---

[4] See Chap. III.

To Help in the Solution of Problems. Worship, with its presentation of new visions, its opportunity for recollection and meditation,[5] its stimulation of new impulses through the eternal quest for God, ought to help the worshiper to find the solution to his problems of living. If worship is to aid the worshiper to receive God's help in the solution of his problems, he must first feel that he *has* a problem. Sometimes worship serves the double function of revealing the problem and of aiding in the solution.

A young woman during a worship service based on the theme of "Awareness" was suddenly arrested by that section of the service which stressed "Awareness of the fine possibilities in other people." She had been finding it increasingly difficult to adjust herself harmoniously to a member of her family group. What was the leader of worship saying?

> "Who art thou, O Spirit of Man?
> Thou art the Child of the Infinite;
> In thy nostrils is the breath of God."

She thrilled at the majesty of the thought. But the leader was now reading the poem "Souls." She had come to the last verse:

> "And folk, whose earth-stained looks I hate,
> Why may I not divine
> Your Souls, that must be passionate,
> Shining and swift, as mine!"[6]

Then followed a few moments of silence for meditation, and in that silence the "Awareness" came to this worshiper. Was that her real problem after all? Not the need to adjust herself to an unpleasant personality, but

---

[5] See Chap. I, "Aims of Worship."
[6] From "Souls," by Fannie Stearns Davis, found in *Myself and I*. The Macmillan Company, New York. Used by permission.

the need to discern in that other personality a soul "shining and swift"? In an experience like this worship both revealed the problem and suggested a solution as well.

At other times the problem will have to be revealed to the group or the individual in a period of preparation, used expressly for this purpose. Sometimes the class period provides the opportunity to make the group conscious of the problem.

To Meet Certain Universal Needs. In building a worship program we must keep in mind the fact that there are certain universal needs which are fundamental in the lives of all people. A study of the immediate situations in our groups may not reveal a continuous succession of problems of equally vital importance. There are home, school, play, church, community, or world situations in which most people find themselves at some time or other and in which they are called upon to live as children of God and followers of Jesus. Doctor Hartshorne a number of years ago defined these relationships as those of gratitude, good will, loyalty, reverence, and faith. They are indicative of what some of these universal relationships to God and men may be.

We do not want certain immediately pressing situations in the group life to loom so large that we fail to discern some of these universal experiences which every group needs at one time or another. Any group at times in its worship should practice the presence of God and feel itself strengthened in those great reassurances that God is and that they may commune with him. Every group needs at some time to face in worship the challenge of living life on its higher levels or of meeting the crying need for social justice. So, as we select themes for worship, we must see that these universal needs are met, as well as those very specific ones which emerge constantly in the life of any group.

To Afford an Opportunity for the Expression of Interests and Desires. Not only in moments of need does man turn to God, but there wells up within him the desire to share with God those high moments of joy and appreciation which characterize every well-balanced life. Children, young people, and adults all have certain absorbing interests into which they throw their whole personalities. There are desires and urges, many of them splendid and uplifting, which make life inestimably beautiful when we share them with God in worship. There are happy experiences which we may relive in a service of worship and thus imbue them with a deeper significance. It is natural, then, that some of the worship services be based on themes which will afford an opportunity for the expression of appreciation.

To Associate God With Everyday Activities. We have noted the growing feeling that the environment of worship itself ought to suggest its vital relationship to life and its great interests.[7] The worshiper wants to feel that while he is, in a sense, leaving the perplexities of life behind, when he enters the place of worship, yet he will find there a richer, deeper meaning for all of those pressing life activities which claim his strength and attention every day.

Why work with all the strength of one's life at a given task? For what end? How play, so that all of the finer ideals of living may be kept intact? Family life, with its interrelationships of personalities, the arena in which so many battles for character must be fought—

---

[7] Chap. II.

how raise it to the level of God-companionship? Our
vocations—are we working alone or may we feel the
companionship of another worker at our side? Our
worship objectives may be chosen at times with the
definite purpose of making a sacrament of life's everyday activities.

To Make Our Festival Days Days of God-Communion.
Among life's natural interests are certain great festival days which occur regularly and which need ever
new interpretations to give them meaning. Some of
these recurring festivals find their origin in the Church
Year, such as Christmas, Epiphany, and Easter. Others,
like Thanksgiving, celebrate national events. Some
find their sanction in international or world-wide meanings. They may be observed perfunctorily and without enriching the worship experience, or they may
from year to year be treated with new approaches and
supply a variety of themes for worship. The Thanksgiving festival, coming in a year of depression and world
disaster, needs to have a new interpretation if some
through their worship are not to express unthinking
gratification for immunity from suffering, while others
in resentment at life's injustices refuse to worship at all.
Christmas in the children's departments of the church
may repeat each year the emphasis of gratitude for the
baby Jesus; or deeper insights into its significance can
be opened up to boys and girls by emphasizing the significance of Jesus' life. We celebrate the birthdays of
most great men not because they were born as babies
but because of the contribution of their lives. The
Christmas festival, even for boys and girls, can be
fraught with far greater significance than is often
accorded it.

GUIDING THE EXPERIENCE OF WORSHIP

To Provide a Continuity in the Worship Experience.
Worship, like all of life, should be a growing experience.
The aims of worship chosen for any group in the church
school should have in mind carrying the worshipers
during a year from one level of worship experience
to higher and higher levels. There should be real growth
in Christian character, and worship should help to contribute to this growth. There should be a gradual enrichment of our concepts of God. And, above all else,
there should be a growing experience of real companionship with God.

In selecting worship objectives this developing experience of living, growing personalities should be kept in
mind. To be sure that Christian character is being
formed and that there is an opportunity for real growth,
it is advisable to plan worship, to meet certain definite
objectives for a consecutive number of Sundays. The
individual needs the opportunity to actually work out
the worship ideal in life. He needs the repeated stimulation which worship gives to practice the new relationship to God which the worship objective is stressing.

For how long in advance shall one plan the themes
of worship? There is no one answer to this question in
a way which is applicable in all situations. The danger
of a worship program which is outlined in detail for a
year in advance is that the program, as set up, may
inhibit flexibility in adapting it to suddenly emerging
needs. Yet one of the most flexible and creative worship
programs I have ever seen was planned for a school year
around the central theme, "The Quest for God." This
was sufficiently broad to allow for all sorts of adapta-
tions to meet interests and problems as they came up
in the group life. There is an advantage in thinking

ahead in terms of a worship program that shall lead from one experience to another, provided this planning is not so rigid that it cannot be altered or even changed radically if the problems or interests which arise in a group indicate more urgent needs which must be met.

Selecting Objectives in an Integrated Curriculum. The ideal type of curriculum is that in which worship is not thought of as an experience set off from the class discussions and the activity projects which a department is carrying on, but as an integral part of a total experience which all are sharing. In those church schools, not yet large in number, in which each grade meets separately, this type of integrated curriculum is possible. This is also true of departments which are using a series of group-graded curriculum materials, for the worship services may be on themes closely related to the class activities.

This type of worship is most easily possible when the curriculum is developed from the urgent needs and interests of any group. Here is a group of Juniors, in the fall of the year, using a textbook which includes for the Sundays preceding Thanksgiving the familiar stories of the landing of the Pilgrims. Their teacher is attempting to tell them about the Pilgrims in Holland. The girls, a class of ten nine-year-olds, know the story as well as, if not better than, their teacher. They have had it in public school, and they know far more details than the church-school textbook supplies. They interrupt the telling of the story, they are restless, eager to tell it themselves. Suddenly, in a pause, Elsie asks, "Did you ever stop to think what we would be if the Pilgrim Fathers had stayed in Holland?"

Ruth: Maybe we'd be Dutch.

Elsie: But, what I really want to know is how the first man got here. Did God make him a big man? Or was he a little baby? And if he was a baby, how did he get here, and who took care of him? That's the only question I want to know.

(The whole group of girls became alert in an instant.)

Several Girls: Yes, we'd like to know that too.

Mary: I saw a picture once of the first man. There was a house and a grown-up man in the picture.

Teacher: Did you think that was a true picture of what really happened, Mary?

Mary: No, I thought it was funny.

Ruth: Well, I asked my mother and she said she didn't know. Elsie, wouldn't your uncle know?

(This uncle was a visitor, evidently quite a personage, as Ruth had been pointing him out to the other girls.)

Elsie: Oh, mercy, no, he wouldn't know. Just because he traveled around the world is no sign that he'd know the answer to a question like that.

Teacher: There is a book in the children's room at the library called *The World We Live in and How It Came to Be.* I think we could find at least the beginning of an answer to your question in it. It has pictures too of how the world may have looked way back in the beginning. I will see if I can bring the book next Sunday, and suppose we spend several weeks trying to find the answer to your question.

Elsie: Well, we don't want any made-up stories. *We want the truth.*

Several Girls: Yes, we want the truth.

Now, let us imagine this group of girls with its curriculum for the next weeks centered in trying to find an answer to this question so vital to them, carrying on research to find a solution to their problem, delving back into the mystery surrounding the beginnings of things. If they must meet for worship in a department with a number of other grades, there will be little opportunity to make worship an integral part of their program, except for a brief few minutes in their class period.

But if this Junior Department were organized by grades, this fourth grade meeting with its teacher, for the entire program of religious education, then, as they explored their problem, they could worship together at those moments when the sense of mystery and wonder needed expression in worship. As they pushed farther and farther back into the beginnings of things and began to feel the power of eternal laws and identified the on-going creative process as God, they might begin to feel a sense of security in the thought that this God of all the ages was the very same God with whom they could share companionship. Through worship services they could feel themselves one with God through endless years of growth. The worship program for this group would be an integral part of their whole experience.

This same type of integrated worship experience is possible for any adolescent group whose total curriculum experience is a unit, research, study, activity, and worship all developing out of and ministering to some problem or need or interest of the group.

But it is also possible to achieve a certain amount of integration, even when the groups within a department are following out different interests. This is accomplished by bringing these groups together to share some common enterprises and to become conscious of their fellowship through sharing with each other their separate group interests. This type of fellowship through worship requires more than a sixty-minute church-school period, for there must be time in which the different classes can talk with each other and work together. In such cases the worship grows out of the values and ideals which all come to appreciate or out of some problem or enterprise which has developed out of this interclass fellowship.

How to Use Printed Worship Guides

Many church workers will feel that they are not sufficiently experienced to build a worship program based entirely upon the discovery of their own group needs. Many leaders will find it difficult to follow the emerging interests of their groups and at the same time plan a well-balanced program. All of us need, from time to time, the stimulation of the thought of others, that our imaginations may be kindled to glimpse new ways of enriching our services of worship.

For all of these reasons it is advisable to be familiar with the increasing number of printed worship guides which are available. These can be secured from denominational headquarters; they are to be found in denominational and interdenominational magazines of religious education; and some of them are published in book form. Often these contain descriptions of the way in which one group arrived at its worship objectives, so that the reader can obtain valuable help in how to go to work to discover his own group needs.

Gaining Suggestions for Worship Objectives. One use of such printed worship guides is to suggest to us certain worship objectives which we may have overlooked in planning the program for our group. A beginner in the leadership of worship may have to depend more upon such help than he will after he has had some experience in discovering worship needs.

Gaining Help to Meet Specific Needs. Let us suppose that a leader had in his church group Harriet and her friends who were in doubt about the efficacy of prayer. He need not feel that he must create entirely original worship services to meet this need. Nor need he disregard the situation altogether because he does not feel adequate to discovering appropriate worship materials or defining all the necessary objectives. He can turn to some book of worship services for young people and find there a series on prayer which may be rich in suggestions for his own situation. Or in some issue of a denominational or interdenominational magazine he may find worship services based on this theme. He need not follow each service slavishly, just as it is printed, but make such alterations in it as will adapt it to meet his requirements.

Studying the Principles of Worship Building in Printed Worship Guides. One of the best ways to become familiar with the theory as well as the practice of worship building is to study the published materials and attempt to discover how the principles of creative worship have been followed in the creating of these services.

Learning Through Using Guides Prepared by Others. For many beginners in the art of planning and conducting worship it will be best to adopt some good worship guide as a basis for their worship program, and then, through its use, to learn gradually how to deviate from its suggestions or how to alter them to suit their own group interests and needs. It is important that the vital needs of any group take precedence over any printed program, and that when materials prepared by others are used, it should be done with the utmost flexibility.

Discovering Worship Materials. A leader may be very creative in building a worship program, in the selection of his objectives and in the general plan of procedure, and yet need constant enrichment through the discovery of new worship materials. Leaders of worship will want to be familiar with all the best that are published by denominational houses and others in order that the services of worship may remain fresh and vital.

ADDITIONAL READING SOURCES

Athearn, Laura Armstrong, *Christian Worship for American Youth*. D. Appleton-Century Company.

Baker, Edna Dean, *The Worship of the Little Child*. The Methodist Book Concern.

Blashfield, Clara Beers, *Worship Training for Primary Children*. The Methodist Book Concern.

Brown, Arthur H., *Worship* (pamphlet in the series, *Everyday Adventures in Christian Living*). The Methodist Book Concern.

Carrier, Blanche, *How Shall I Learn to Teach Religion?* Harper & Brothers.

Eakin, Mildred Moody, *Teaching Junior Boys and Girls*. The Abingdon Press.

Forest, Ilse, *Child Life and Religion*. Harper & Brothers.

Gates, Sherwood, *Youth at Worship*. (Christian Quest Pamphlet No. 6.) International Council of Religious Education.

Geer, Owen M., *Adventures in the Devotional Life*. Board of Education of the Methodist Episcopal Church.

Harris, Thomas L., *Christian Public Worship*. Harper & Brothers.

Hartshorne, Hugh, *Manual for Training in Worship*. Charles Scribner's Sons.

Jones, Mary Alice, *Training Juniors in Worship*. Cokesbury Press.

Perkins, Ruth, *Planning Services of Worship*. The Woman's Press.

Powell, Marie Cole, *Junior Method in the Church School*. The Abingdon Press.

Rex, Ruth Erwin, *We Worship: Services of Worship for the Small Church School*. D. Appleton-Century Company.

Shaver, E. L., and Stock, H. T., *Training Young People in Worship*. The Pilgrim Press.

Shaver, E. L., *Youth and Worship* (Course 15 in the High School Leadership Curriculum). The Pilgrim Press.

Books Containing Worship Services

Athearn, Laura Armstrong, *Christian Worship for American Youth*. D. Appleton-Century Company.

Burgess, Nellie G., *Junior Worship Materials*. Cokesbury Press.

Crandall, Edna, *A Curriculum of Worship for the Junior Church School*. D. Appleton-Century Company.

Hartshorne, Hugh, *Manual for Training in Worship*. Charles Scribner's Sons.

Hartshorne, Hugh, *Stories for Worship and How to Follow Them Up*. Charles Scribner's Sons.

Jones, Charlotte Chambers, *Junior Worship Guide*. The Pilgrim Press.

Mattoon and Bragdon, *Services for the Open*. D. Appleton-Century Company.

Perkins, Jeannette E., *Primary Worship Guide*. The Pilgrim Press.

Pickett, Warren Wheeler, *Worship Services for Young People*. The Pilgrim Press.

Oxford University Press, *The Kingdom, the Power and the Glory*. Humphrey Milford, London.

Shaver, E. L., *Church School Projects*. University of Chicago Press.

Stacy, Gussie Brown, *Worship for Youth*. Powell and White.

The International Journal of Religious Education. Current issues contain suggestions for building worship services for all departments of the church school.

Consult also denominational magazines, pamphlets and hymnals.

Books Describing Worship Experience

Carrier, Blanche, and Clowes, Amy, *Building a Christian Character*. Harper & Brothers.

Carrier, Blanche, and Clowes, Amy, *Seeking the Beautiful in God's World*. Harper & Brothers.

Danielson, Frances W., and Perkins, Jeannette E., *Teaching Without Textbooks*. The Pilgrim Press.

Hartshorne, Hugh, and Lotz, Elsa, *Case Studies of Present-Day Religious Teaching*. Yale University Press.

Sweet, Blanche Furman, and Fahs, Sophia Lyon, *Exploring Religion With Eight Year Olds*. Henry Holt & Co.

Watson, Goodwin, *Case Studies for Teachers of Religion*. Association Press.

Perkins, Jeannette, *Others Call It God*. Harper & Brothers.

Perkins, Jeannette, *As Children Worship*. The Pilgrim Press.

CHAPTER V

THE SERVICE OF WORSHIP

Each service of worship when it takes place in a given congregation is a new event in the lives of the members and in the life of the leader. . . .

When you realize that in a congregation of a hundred there are a hundred souls each of whom has arrived at a particular moment in his earthly pilgrimage; that that particular moment marks also a certain definite milestone in the life-experience of the leader; that the exact stage of development of the news of the day, or current history, is something that it has never been before and will never be precisely again—then you understand that each and every service represents a unique concatenation of individual and social psychic states: a combination that exists "now and never again," and which is here and now offered to God as a new, an unrepeatable sacrifice. If leaders of worship would prepare each service in this mood, and if worshipers would approach every act of churchgoing in this spirit, there would never be such a thing as a "lifeless" service.—JOHN W. SUTER.

Open Doors in Religious Education, pp. 18-19. Harper & Brothers, publishers.

FOR whatever age group we are planning worship services the principles which will guide us are the same. The differences will come in the life situations, the interests and capacities of the age groups for which worship is being planned and variations in methods of procedure to meet all these differences.

It is important for any leader to understand the following principles of worship planning. For, even though he uses worship suggestions prepared by others, he will want to be able to select wisely. As he sees well-built services of worship worked out by others in accordance with these principles, he may gradually acquire the technique of using them himself in a more creative way.

PRINCIPLES OF CREATIVE WORSHIP

Worship is very closely related to the arts. It is often spoken of as "The Art of Worship." A perfect worship service is a work of art, and as such involves an act of creation. But, like all creative arts, it produces its cumulative effect by adherence to certain underlying principles, a knowledge of which constitutes the artist's craft. Often a worship service may reveal spots of beauty, but, as a whole, be marred by other parts which are out of relation to the whole.

This is as true of some of the simpler and less formal types of worship services as it is of the Sunday-morning worship service of the adult congregation. The beauty of the same principles may shine through the simplest service. Sometimes the simpler the form the more difficult the craftsmanship.

The Principle of Unity. Any great work of art has a central message or mood which gives it unity. All details are subordinated to this central idea; all details are deliberately chosen to emphasize or reveal this central unity. So, in planning a service of worship all the materials should be selected to emphasize the objective of the service.

We are concerned in worship building with both the unity of thought and the unity of feeling. The following worship service reveals a fine adherence to the principle of unity of thought. All the materials, from the introductory emphasis by the leader through the hymns, the talk, the picture interpretation and the prayer, express the central thought of the service, "The Power of a Deathless Life." Of the great mass of material available about Lincoln, only that which brings out this quality in his life is used in this service.

I. The Occasion—Lincoln's Birthday.

II. The Situation:

This service was one in a series to help the group feel that there is an eternal quality about lives which are lived on the plane of high ideals. The one following it, celebrating Washington's Birthday, had its central message in Mary Antin's story, "The Lie." This is the story of the influence of the ideals of Washington upon one small Jewish boy in the American public school, but more especially of the spiritual understanding and deathless influence of the boy's sympathetic school-teacher.

Before the group on an easel stood a beautiful colored reproduction of Eastman Johnson's painting, "The Young Lincoln Reading."

III. The Theme: "The Power of a Deathless Life."

Introduction by Leader:

Was it Saint Augustine who once said, "One loving heart may set another on fire"? Robert Speer has written a life of that remarkable girl, Alice Jackson, who died while she was still young, but who had already touched with a quickening fire the lives of hundreds of college and working girls. The little book is called *One Girl's Influence.*

Probably all of you can think at this moment of someone whom you have known whose life had this deathless quality about it. I am thinking at this moment of the young woman who was the public librarian in our community for many years. She did more than hand out books across that counter. She touched us with some living quality. In how many of us she aroused enthusiasms for good books! How many young people lingered to hear about her last hike to the woods as they buried their faces in the great cluster of woodsy things she had placed on the book counter! What vistas of creative living she opened up to all who came! Shall I ever forget that morning when she leaned across and quoted to the college professor who was raising doubts about immortality those immortal words of Emily Dickinson's poem, "Chartless"?[1]

This librarian died, still young, after a long illness filled with unutterable suffering. But during that illness no tears were allowed in that sick room. "It is the beginning of life's greatest adventure," she said.

Since her death I never enter the library and stand before the pot of growing flowers which is always there in the spot where she always kept flowers, that I am not vividly conscious of her presence. As I stand there I sometimes think of a song called "I Love Life." She loved life, and she lives forever.

Some lives have this deathless quality. Lincoln is one of those who lives on in the interests and enthusiasms of many. I am thinking of one great Lincoln-lover whom I knew personally, of his tireless, eager efforts to trace down some bit of information about Lincoln, of his kindling enthusiasm when in some little mountain town his search was

---

[1] See *The Complete Poems of Emily Dickinson*, pp. 188-189.

rewarded. In remembrance of such deathless lives, we invite you to sing:

Hymn:

"To thee, Eternal Soul, be praise,
Who from of old to our own days,
Through souls of saints and prophets, Lord,
Hast sent thy light, thy love, thy word."[2]

Talk: "What Lincoln Has Meant to Me." (By a young man who is a great admirer of Lincoln.)

Interpretation of Picture:

Statement about the place where the picture hangs in the library of Berea College, Kentucky. The appropriateness of this picture in that spot, suggesting the possible influence of the young mountaineer, Abe Lincoln, over other young mountaineers eager for an education. In the picture the young Lincoln is being influenced through his books by other men who have lived before him.

Solo: "Father Abraham."[3]

Prayer: Of thanksgiving for the courage and assurance which such deathless lives give us; of appreciation for that communion of saints which links us to them; of aspiration that we, too, may love life, that we may live it richly and vividly, that we may live it for others and so gain that deathless quality which lives on in the lives of others; of joy in the possibility of companionship with the living Christ who said, "I am come that ye might have life and have it more abundantly."

---

[2] By Richard Watson Gilder, from *American Student Hymnal.* Copyright of poem owned by Houghton Mifflin Company. Used by permission.
[3] Found in *Services for the Open.* D. Appleton-Century Company.

Hymn: "Pass On the Torch."[4]

"Pass on the torch, pass on the flame;
Remember whence the Glory came,
And eyes are on you as you run,
Beyond the shining of the sun!

"Lord Christ, we take the torch from thee!
We must be true, we will be free;
And clean of heart and strong of soul,
To bear the glory to its goal.

"America, God hear the prayer—
America for God! We dare,
With Lincoln's heart and Lincoln's hand,
To fling a flame across the land!

"O Lord of life, to thee we kneel;
Maker of men, our purpose seal!
We will, for honor of thy name,
Pass on the torch, pass on the flame!"

Unity of feeling is sustained, in part, by the leader and his ability to emphasize the dominant emotional tone of the service. But the selection and arrangement of materials will also further this end. The mood of the service in remembrance of Lincoln is predominantly one of triumph and aspiration. The introduction by the leader struck this note which was sustained by the victorious mood of the solo as well as by the closing hymn of dedication.

Services of worship are made more effective too by adherence to literary and artistic unity. In a service built around the early life of Emily Dickinson, emphasizing her many friendly acts, the call to worship was selected from the works of some other poet. Since the entire service was based on the life of Emily Dickinson,

---

[4] By Allan Eastman Cross, from *The American Student Hymnal.*
Also, *New Hymnal for American Youth.* Used by permission.

artistic unity would be secured by using as a call to worship her lovely poem:

> "If I can stop one heart from breaking,
>   I shall not live in vain;
> If I can ease one life the aching,
>   Or cool one pain,
> Or help one fainting robin
>   Into his nest again,
>   I shall not live in vain."[5]

Similarly, in a service emphasizing the influence of nature upon the soul of man and its power to draw man Godward, and featuring the life of Saint Francis of Assisi, artistic unity is observed by using his own great hymn, "All Creatures of Our God and King."

In children's groups informal worship is often characterized by a strong feeling of unity for the very reason that it has come as an answer to some felt need on the part of the group and so in a very direct way helps to meet that need. When the kindergarten children found on their table one Sunday morning a box of woodsy things brought to them by their pastor returning from his vacation, and Zona Maie remarked with quiet happiness, "He didn't forget us while he was away," and when another child said, "I feel like saying, 'Every morning seems to say,'" the principle of unity was inherent in the worship situation.

> "Every morning seems to say
>   There's something happy on the way
>   And God sends love to you."

sang the children, while one after another they gathered around the vase of woodsy things.

[5] From *The Complete Poems of Emily Dickinson*, p. 6, Centenary Edition. Edited by Martha Dickinson, Bianchi and Alfred Leete Hamson. Reprinted by permission of Little, Brown & Company.

"What shall we say to the Heavenly Father this morning?" asked the teacher, joining them.

"Thank you for the things from the woods," said George.

"Thank you for making Mr. B. think about bringing them to us," added Flody.[6]

And so the teacher voiced their prayers, and in a very spontaneous worship experience the principle of unity was observed.

The Principle of Emphasis. If we read carefully what any number of writers have to say about what goes on in worship,[7] we shall see that all of the descriptions of the worship process imply, if they do not directly state, a crescendo of experience. The worship service rises by steps to a high point of insight. Or it may be said to proceed from one experience to another, each one carrying us further along in our communion with God. Some writers speak of the worship service as having a climax, like a story.[8]

Occasionally the offertory is spoken of as the climax, because it is an opportunity for the worshiper to do something as a result of his worship experience. But the offertory is not necessarily the spiritual climax of a worship service. In fact, in many worship services the offertory is in no sense the climax. In a series of services planned to stimulate the joy of giving, the offertory would be the natural climax of the worship service in that every other part of the service would lead up to the act of giving.

In many services the prayer is the climax, for it is

---

[6] From *Teaching Without Textbooks*, by Danielson and Perkins, pp. 23-24. Copyright, The Pilgrim Press. Used by permission.
[7] See Appendix A.
[8] See Mary Alice Jones, *Training Juniors in Worship*, Chap. XI, p. 169.

through the prayer that the worshiper voices his new resolves, his aspirations, his dedication to living God's life in the world. This is one reason for placing the prayer more often toward the close of the worship service.

On some occasions a unison prayer may come earlier in the service to prepare the group for worship, to help us to feel God's nearness, and the climax may come in some hymn of dedication which closes the service. Then, again, both *prayer and hymn* together may be the climax.

It may be helpful to think of a worship service as being divided into four main divisions, each division marking one of four progressive steps in the act of worship. These divisions for the sake of simplicity may be classified as:

I. THE BEGINNING OR PREPARATION

This may include some or all of the following:

(a) *An opening Prelude.*

The Prelude may be an act of preparation for worship in that it induces a mood of quiet thoughtfulness, or a releasing of tension, or the forgetfulness of life's frictions. Often the Prelude is selected to emphasize the theme of the service. In a service of rejoicing over the awakening life of springtime, music on spring themes will prepare the group at the very opening of the service for what is to follow.

(b) *The opening Hymn.*

The first hymn is sometimes a processional and sometimes a congregational hymn. It too may prepare the worshiper by its emphasis upon the theme of the service.

(c) The Call to Worship.

The call to worship may be given by the leader or it may be in the nature of responses between the leader and the group. Often these responses are musical in character. Some groups use the same call to worship for all services. While it may be wise in some situations to use the same call to worship for a series of services, it is well to remember that much repetition is apt to render meaningless any part of the worship service, so that one form, used repeatedly, may cease to be a real call to worship. Then, too, a service of challenge requires a different type of call to worship from a service of quiet meditation.

The call to worship often gains force and vitality if it at the same time directs attention to the theme for the day. In a service on the theme, "With God in This Mysterious Universe," the following might be substituted for a call to worship, and would not only be emphasizing the theme, but would be preparing the worshiper by inducing the attitude of wonder:

> "A little thing is our earth,
> Slung, by a thread unseen,
> In a tiny trail round a lesser star;
> Beyond it—Infinitude.
> Universe beyond universe,
> Bright, estranged, unknowable.
>
> .   .   .   .
>
> A little thing is our earth
> And beyond it is Infinitude."[9]

(d) An opening Prayer.

The opening prayer, as an act of preparation, may be offered by the leader or it may be a unison prayer by

---

[9] From *The Sacraments of Common Life*, by J. S. Hoyland, p. 23. W. Heffer & Sons, Ltd., London. Used by permission.

the group. In content it may cover general petitions, aiding the worshipers to feel God's nearness, to express their desire for forgiveness, or to look forward with expectancy to the worship experience. On the other hand, this opening prayer may relate more specifically to the theme of the service.

II. PRESENTATION AND DEVELOPMENT

This section of the worship service may include a variety of materials. Since most of these elements of worship are discussed in following chapters, only brief reference is made to them here. Naturally, not all of the following will be incorporated in any one service, but a selection will be made from among these:

(a) A story or talk. (b) Conversation. (c) Dramatic presentation of truth. (d) Picture appreciation. (e) Scripture. (f) Selections from prose or poetry. (g) Responsive readings. (h) Hymns. (i) Anthems or solos.

There is no set rule as to the order in which these elements shall occur when more than one is used. Scripture precedes more often than follows the story or talk, but there are occasions when the Scripture might be given new meaning by being placed later in the service. One can imagine that *after* a vivid story-talk on Kagawa with the emphasis upon his book, *Love, the Law of Life,* the worshiping group would repeat the thirteenth chapter of First Corinthians with far more spiritual insight and a deeper emotional response than they would had it preceded the illustrative material.

III. CLIMAX AND CONSUMMATION

Ideally the worshipers themselves should have some opportunity to express the newly roused resolves which the worship service has stimulated. This they may do through unison prayer and response and through the singing of a hymn. Sometimes the leader voices this expression for the group in a prayer carefully selected or prepared for the occasion. In some instances both types of expression are used. In one church, after the minister has closed his sermon with a prayer, the congregation unites in the following act of dedication. The entire closing section of this worship service is printed, including the collect for consecration.[10]

The Sermon.

Prayer. (By the minister.)

A Collect for Consecration:

Since it is of thy mercy, O gracious Father, that another day is added to our lives; we here dedicate both our souls and our bodies to thee and thy service, in a sober, righteous, and godly life: in which resolution do thou, O merciful God, confirm and strengthen us; that, as we grow in age, we may grow in grace, and in the knowledge of our Lord and Saviour Jesus Christ.

The Choir Response.

The Benediction.

Recessional.

Silent Prayer.

* * * * *

The various vehicles for the climax of worship are:
(*a*) Prayer, individual or unison; spoken or silent. (*b*) Prayer responses. (*c*) A hymn. (*d*) An expres-

[10] The morning worship of the Second Church in Newton, Congregational, Rev. Boynton P. Merrill, pastor.

sion of resolve or aspiration. (*e*) A musical number by a soloist or choir. (*f*) A period of silence, allowing for individual thinking about the outcome of the worship service. (*g*) The offertory.

IV. BENEDICTION

Not all of the necessarily brief services which are held in the church school require a formal benediction. But, there are times when it aids in rounding out the service to a more artistic and satisfying conclusion. Many services may close with the act of dedication as the climax of the worship service. The benediction if used may take the form of:

(*a*) A benediction by the leader. (*b*) A unison benediction. (*c*) A musical response. (*d*) A combination of these forms.

So the art of planning worship includes not only preserving the unity of the service, but also the most effective arrangement and order of the different materials. There is possible some variety of arrangement from time to time while we still preserve the principles of unity and emphasis.

The Principle of Creativity. What has been said about the principle of emphasis reveals the opportunity which exists for creative planning of worship programs. It is well for any leader to familiarize himself with the great traditional forms of worship and surrender himself to an appreciation of their beauty. Then he should attempt to understand what happens to the worshiper psychologically during the act of worship.[11] Equipped with this experience, he is prepared to think of the age needs of his group as well as their background and

---

[11] See Chaps. I and II.

interests, and to find a form or pattern for worship which will best meet those needs and interests. He will probably discover the value of experimenting with different forms for different types of worship experiences. A service of meditation will adapt itself to some forms better than others. A nature service may suggest quite another form. A service of dedication will develop along lines determined by the very nature of its purpose and content.

There is need for a more creative treatment of the content of worship as well as its forms. This will be considered in the chapters dealing with materials of worship.

It must be remembered that there is a vast difference between being truly creative in planning worship and adopting fads or features because someone else has used them. To include a salute to the flag in every worship service regardless of its character or purpose is not creative. But, neither is it an indication of the creative spirit to introduce a symbolic candle-lighting service just because another leader has used it effectively, regardless of the existence of a genuine group experience for which candle light stands as a symbol. Real creativity is possible only when there is a background of understanding of the meaning of worship, its psychological basis, and the laws governing its effective functioning.

The Principle of Variation. Truly creative planning of worship recognizes this law of variation. Services of worship which remain year after year, or month after month, practically unchanged in form or content gradually lose their power to stir the soul of the worshiper. Of this law Dearmer says, "Again let me insist on what the psychologist knows so well, that variation lies at the heart of attention and therefore of all fervor in worship."[12]

Many of us will find it more practical to vary the content than the form of worship. This is one reason why those responsible for worship should have a wide acquaintance with a variety of worship materials. But most of us can at times vary even the form of worship. Some worship services may be far more ritualistic than others. There are services largely given over to silence or to meditation accompanied by music. Occasionally the drama may be the medium through which a group worships. Even within a simple form which is followed in brief departmental services in the church school there is opportunity for variation in the placing of the prayer or in the arrangement of other materials in the service. Silent prayer, unison prayer and the Litany all provide for variation in form and content. Even those of us who lean toward a most conservative use of this law of variation will be interested to read about some experiments which others are carrying on in the way of using new forms for worship.[13]

---

[12] *The Art of Public Worship*, p. 103. Morehouse Publishing Company. Used by permission.
[13] See Guthrie, *The Offices of Mystical Religion*. Also article in the *International Journal of Religious Education*, May, 1933, "A Ritual in Rhythm," by Nancy Longenecker.

CHAPTER VI

MATERIALS OF WORSHIP

When this vision dawns on man, it arouses in him a desire not only to approve, but to respond. He has the immediate sense of a Vision, which something within urges him to translate into action. . . .

The revelation of God himself, when it flashes on man as a thing eminently desirable, stimulates to imitation. Man seeks to be like God, even if with fear and trembling. He would fain live the life that he would approve.—A. S. DUNCAN-JONES.

From *The Necessity of Art,* by Dearmer and others, Student Christian Movement, London.

THE materials of worship have varied with different ages and races. There was a time when the dance and the drama were the vehicles through which men expressed their religious feelings. Offerings of the fruits of the fields, and sacrifices of burnt offerings have been the symbols of man's relationship to God among many races. Chants and songs early conveyed the worshiper's aspirations Godward, and a rich and colorful liturgy has interpreted the vision of God to men in some communions.

The materials of worship have been wide and varied. And they still may be—for, whatever will interpret the inner meaning of our relationship to God, whatever will clothe the vision with beauty and desirability, that may become material for the expression of worship.

PURPOSE OF WORSHIP MATERIALS

To Focus Attention. The materials of worship serve a number of purposes. One purpose is to focus the attention of the worshiper upon the meaning of the service and thus create a sense of reality. Attention is a precondition of participation in worship. Attention with a sense of concern will carry the worshiper through the service in a state of mental activity, which means that he will receive benefit from it. To secure this kind of attention, the materials of worship must be chosen to meet the group and individual needs and must be adapted to the age capacity of the members of the group.

To Interpret the Worship Objective. Another purpose of the worship material is to interpret the worship objective to the worshiper. Children, especially, need to have this interpretation made very clear. The adult who enters a place of worship and begins to participate in the service soon senses the significance of it because of his wide experience and because of the many associations built up around the meanings of the worship materials.

The child, on the other hand, is living life objectively. He is not much given to interpretation. He is too busy living life to have much time or inclination to reflect upon it. The associations which he has built up around ideals are few and not well organized. Therefore the materials of worship must very clearly interpret to him the ideals which the service is emphasizing.

To Visualize the Worship Ideal. Through the materials of worship the vision of God and of the possibilities of living as God's child and in companionship with him must flash upon the worshiper. Sometimes the materials of worship will actually visualize the significance of worship through art forms, as in pictures or the drama.

To Provide Opportunity for Expression of the Wor-

ship Feeling. Of all the functions of worship materials, none is more important than that of affording the worshiper an opportunity to express his feeling of fellowship with God. The materials of worship should be selected with this purpose always in mind—to secure the utmost of participation by the worshiping group.

STORY MATERIAL IN WORSHIP

Since the effectiveness of the story as an educational method is being re-examined to-day, and since so much of its possible effectiveness depends upon the way in which it is used, it is important to see what the function of a story is and how its function may help to fulfill the purposes of worship.

The Function of the Story in Worship. The story has power to visualize an ideal or a great truth lived out in concrete situations. The younger we are, the less able are we to comprehend abstract ideas, such as courage, loyalty, helpfulness. But children can thrill to a brave action; they can recognize a helpful person. "I saw helpness, this very morning," said primary-age Henry. "I saw it when my mother was trying to help my little sister be nice." Even as we grow older, the story-presentation of abstract truths has a vividness and an appeal which mere talking about them can never have.

Another function of the story is its power to arouse desires and to stimulate emotion. As we listen, we identify ourselves with the characters in the story. We share their purposes and their feelings; for the time being we *live* in the story. If the desires and purposes aroused are noble ones, our emotional natures are enriched by the experience.

Because of its vividness and concreteness a story may

be the means of opening up or restating some challenging problem which needs worship to aid in its solution. Or some group need may be brought before the attention of the group in story form when a more direct statement of this need might not be so effective.

One of the important functions of the story in a worship service is its ability to focus and keep the attention upon the worship theme. The span of child attention is not long, and many an adult finds it difficult to follow, without wandering attention, the sermon which is unrelieved by sufficient illustrative material. How often we forget the text and the main points of the minister's sermons but vividly remember his illustrations!

Because we all enjoy well-told stories, worship which is enriched by the story element tends to become a pleasurable experience. And since one of the purposes of the worship program is to build up pleasurable associations around the experience of worship and thus to help establish the habit of worship, we are justified in using materials which will make worship enjoyable, providing these materials meet all the other standards of value.

Now, although the story may contribute to the worship experience in all these ways, let us see what are some of its limitations. Hartshorne's criticism of the story as a tool for character education is very pertinent at this point. He states that the story may have very harmful results if we enjoy its vicarious action so much that we substitute our pleasurable emotional participation in the vicarious experience for any real action of our own. Since one of the important outcomes of worship is the carry-over into living of the attitudes and ideals stimulated by the worship experience, we shall fail to realize one of our primary aims of worship if members of a worshiping group thrill to the worship ideal set forth in a story and then sit back and do nothing about it. Doctor Hartshorne says, "We can learn soon enough to satisfy our desires for a more perfect state of affairs by contemplating the images aroused by a story without taking the slightest trouble to make them real in fact."[1]

This means that we must not rely upon the story alone to achieve the purposes of worship. Often there needs to be follow-up of the worship story by conversation and discussion and, most important of all, by opportunities for action. When worship is an integral part of group living, then any story material used in connection with the worship experience is apt to be so closely related to the purposeful activity of the group that there is less possibility of this dissociation of worship from conduct.

Selecting Stories for Worship. How shall we make our selection of stories for worship? Some will be discarded because they are too long. Most of us are limited in the time at our disposal for worship and for children's groups the span of child attention limits us still further. Then, too, we do not want the story to overbalance in emphasis the other materials of worship, especially those in which the worshiper expresses his worship feeling.

The first criterion in choosing the story is that it must relate closely to the worship objective. The leader of worship needs a rich background of story material. Every storybook may prove grist for his mill. It may

---

[1] From *Character in Human Relations,* by Hugh Hartshorne, p. 13. Charles Scribner's Sons, New York. Used by permission.

take hours of research to discover just the story which will meet the special need of a particular worship service, but how rewarding after the search to find the story which relates to our objective perfectly! And, during the search, how often we happen upon other stories which we immediately recognize as having possibilities for other occasions! So we get out our story files, and make a record of the story, its theme, the need it might meet, where it is to be found.

We shall want to make sure in our choice of stories that we select those which stimulate Christian motives. The story which always shows virtue rewarded in some material way will give an untrue picture of life. In actual life we often do what is right and we suffer in consequence. But we may find a thrill in the right doing and in the suffering if we feel that by so doing we are working with God. Since motives are so difficult to reach and Christianize,[2] let us make every effort to appeal to only the most worthy ones in worship.

We shall have to discriminate between the fanciful story and the story which is true to life. There is undoubtedly a place for the legendary tale which contains a noble truth beautifully told. But if we desire to have the experience of worship closely tied up with everyday living, a larger number of our stories must deal with situations which are very real ones in the worshiper's experience.

Often there is need of a story emphasis all through a worship service. A brief anecdote told before the singing of a hymn will center the attention upon the words and relate the content of the hymn to the theme of the service. This element of narration, if skillfully used,

---

[2] See *The Motives of Men*, by George Albert Coe.

127

may stimulate the imagination and suggest vivid mental images which will make Scripture responses and prayers more meaningful.

The Talk in the Service of Worship

With little children the story or a conversation is always better than a talk by an adult leader. In adolescent groups, when there begins to be an interest in not only concrete acts of idealism, but in ideals and principles themselves, the talk on the problem uppermost in the worship service may be helpful. Yet, even with adolescent groups, the talk which is generously illustrated by stories is more effective. There is a great deal of the child left in all of us, and most of us are helped by visualizing goodness at work in concrete situations.

Character of the Worship Talk. We must bear in mind one caution, and that is that the talk *for instruction only* belongs in the period of preparation for worship and not in the worship service itself. Any talk used in worship must have as the objective the stimulation of the worship experience. The talk by a returned missionary may be illuminating in its revelation of the customs or attitudes of another race, but it may not be a worship talk. However, if the missionary's talk arouses in us new attitudes of fellowship with the people of another race so that we want to pray for them or to thank God for their fine contribution to the world's culture; if it leads us to desire to co-operate with God in helping them solve their problems, then it rightfully takes its place in worship because it makes us want to worship.

So, the nature talk may be very valuable *educationally*

to the extent that it helps us to understand birds and their habits, or plant life or star constellations. But if that same talk makes us feel that God is behind the great universe of stars, if it leads us to stand in wonder before the beauty and orderliness of God's laws, or if it stimulates us to feel grateful for our Father's world or to be kinder to the animals which he has placed here, then the nature talk is worship material.

All talks, whether given by adults or adolescents, should be concise, well-organized, constructive, not negative, practical yet inspirational, and not a harangue. It is better artistry as well as more profound psychology for the one who is addressing a group to identify himself with them by using the first personal pronoun, *we,* instead of giving the impression that *"I* am exhorting *you* to do something."

There are times when even with the primary or junior children the leader may talk to them for brief moments, sharing with them the results of her richer experience. In such sharing of experience the leader will remember to make her contribution simple without being childish. Children dislike being talked down to. A group of children makes a fine response to the leader who treats them as intelligent human beings, capable of serious and worth-while thinking.

Choice of Language. Language should be concrete in talks to boys and girls, and while we treat their intelligence with respect, we must recognize the limitations of their vocabulary. The words we use should be short and familiar.

Symbolism and Allegory. In talking to boys and girls, symbolism and allegories should be avoided. The child is a literalist. "Opening the doors of his heart to let

Jesus in" means nothing to him, unless it be a very literal picture of the whole proceeding.

One Sunday the minister preached to the children on the text "Benaiah . . . went down also and slew a lion in the midst of a pit in time of snow."[3] The point made was Benaiah's bravery in not being discouraged by the snow, but in braving it to slay the lion. So the children, said the minister, had lions of conduct to slay, and should not be discouraged from attacking and slaying them. The children's group included boys and girls in the kindergarten and primary departments. The *adults* in the congregation greatly enjoyed the *children's* sermon. It is doubtful whether children of this age would identify their conduct-failures with the lion which Benaiah slew. Their interest in the story would be a very concrete one and would certainly be centered in the lion, the snowstorm, and the prowess of the hunter.

Since many ministers and other adults are fond of preaching this sort of allegorical sermon for children, we should note here its probable ineffectiveness as a means of actually changing conduct and of really helping boys and girls to feel God's reality.[4]

Conversation in Worship

At first glance, to the adult who thinks of worship in terms of a formal service moving with finished art toward a climactic ending, the art of conversation may seem entirely too intimate and informal a medium to be associated with worship. Yet there are results which may justify its use, particularly for children's groups

[3] 2 Samuel 23. 20.
[4] See *Religious Education,* December, 1924, "Symposium on Children's Sermons."

and in informal worship experiences for older groups as well.

Advantages of Conversational Material. The advantages of conversation in worship are several. It permits the development of the thought or feeling by the entire group. Each person feels that he has had a part in this. Even those who have not actually said a word, because of the informality of the atmosphere and the fact that the others have contributed and that they *might have,* feel that the period in a certain sense belongs to them and is of their own making.

A second advantage is that conversation creates a sense of fellowship as they work it out together—a fellowship which makes the prayer or hymn which follows a real act of social worship.

The very naturalness of the situation, like countless other moments of conversation in their daily lives, makes worship seem a natural thing and possible in any situation. It removes from the pupil's mind the feeling that worship is something very different from and apart from everyday living. It makes it natural to turn to God for frequent moments of communion.

Often too, by conversation, some worship need is revealed, as the individual answers or asks a question. And often there flowers out of this give-and-take of ideas a spontaneous feeling of worship which a more formal service inhibits. The leader has the opportunity also to know whether the group is really catching the significance of the worship service.

Disadvantages of Conversational Material. Conversation has its disadvantages as well as its values for worship. There is the danger of not keeping to the point. Children are apt to answer the first thing which comes to their minds[5] and the "first thing" may have little bearing upon the worship situation. It is not that the leader is to thrust aside apparently irrelevant answers without sensing that in the child's mind they may have a real bearing on the situation. The leader needs to be sensitive to the unsolved questions, which may be in the background of the child's consciousness. But, if the worship period has been planned to meet a very definite life situation of the group, there will need to be some attempt to guide the conversation to that end.

If the leader is not skilled in the use of the conversational method, he may fail to secure in the conversation answers which are of value for worship. And he may not know what to do with such answers as he does receive.

Sometimes in his effort to guide the conversation toward a definite goal (the objective of worship) the process becomes a forced one. Desired responses are fairly pulled out of the group members or interpretations may be given to their responses which they never meant at all. The result of this ineffective use of conversation is a loss of inspiration and devotional feeling.

How to Use Conversation in Worship. The wise use of this method implies a plan of procedure in the mind of the leader, but a plan not too rigid to allow the utmost of freedom for the group's thinking. It also implies a willingness on the part of the leader to allow worship to take a different trend from the original plan, if the new trend seems to promise to meet the needs of the group. This requires adaptability and consciousness of ability to follow more than one plan.

---

[5] See *The Psychology of Childhood,* by Norsworthy and Whitley, Chap. X, "How Children Think."

Conversation is a method which will be used very largely in periods of preparation for worship, when we are building up attitudes, defining the problem which we desire worship to help us solve, studying hymns, Scripture, prayer for their meanings, or enjoying the appreciation of pictures or music. Used in this way, it will be of service all through the adolescent years, as well as in childhood. But, let us also recognize occasional value right in the worship service itself, even with older boys and girls.

And in the class periods the teacher has a golden opportunity, through informal conversation, to lead his group to the place in their thinking and feeling where expression of newly roused desires in some simple form of class worship is the most natural thing in the world.

DISCUSSION IN WORSHIP

As boys and girls grow older, and are organizing their thinking more thoroughly, conversation often develops into discussion. There have been leaders of adolescent groups who have experimented with the use of discussion in worship.[6]

There is a tendency among adolescents to identify discussion with argumentation. And some leaders, in their effort to secure pupil participation, have consciously pandered to this "love of arguing," inviting it, in order to stimulate class activity.

Real discussion should be an attempt to accumulate all the facts, sincerely to try to understand the other person's point of view and willingness to share one's own thinking without insistence that it is the only right

[6] See *Group Discussion in Religious Education*, by Harrison Elliott, p. 100.

point of view. Discussion of this type is prompted by a real desire to find the best possible solution to the problem, without prejudice.

Argumentation leaves a group divided, with no sense of fellowship and therefore unprepared to worship together. Discussion of the type described above should unite the group in a bond of fellow searchers after the truth and ought to lead the group into the presence of many moments when to worship together seems the inevitable outcome. Discussion which is a sharing process inspires us to sing:

> "Blest be the tie that binds
> Our hearts in Christian love;
> The fellowship of kindred minds
> Is like to that above."

Discussion of this kind is all too rare and may require months of patient experimenting before an adolescent or adult group comes to feel this fellowship of the search after truth. This is the only kind of discussion which leads to worship. Discussion of this type is more easily secured in late adolescent or in adult groups, and every leader of these older groups may have this ideal as a goal before him in his work.

SCRIPTURE IN WORSHIP

In the great religious literature of the world we find help and inspiration to meet our problems. That God-consciousness which throughout the past has helped men to see God's face clearly or to appropriate his strength, may help to stimulate in us awareness of God.

We shall naturally turn to the Bible, our great religious heritage, for such help and inspiration. Mrs. Moulton, in speaking of the Old Testament, says that it is the record of "man with his face toward God." Not always in those early ages when men were groping for and growing into a more adequate religious interpretation of experience was their vision unclouded. But, though ethical insight was dim at times, yet their faces were turned toward God, and throughout the pages of the Old Testament we meet men who lived in the confidence that God's voice was speaking to them. In the New Testament we have the record of One whose whole life was "a practice of the presence of God"; One who, more than any other in the world's history, has spoken with conviction of God's nearness to men and of the possibilities of enriching communion between mankind and God. In a day when men are longing for this reassurance that God lives and that in him we can "live and move and have our being," the Bible ought to furnish worship materials through which men may again voice their search for God and through which they may receive renewed conviction that

> "If I take the wings of the morning,
>   And dwell in the uttermost parts of the sea;
>   Even there shall thy hand lead me,
>   And thy right hand shall hold me."

It seems strange that there is perhaps no one of the materials which needs to be rescued from ineffectiveness more than the biblical material. Its ineffectiveness is owing, not to the material itself, but to the use which is often made of it. Let us see how we can select and use biblical material so that it will enrich the experience of worship.

Selection of Biblical Material for Worship. We shall need to recognize, first of all, that certain parts of the

Bible are worship materials, while others are not. There are homiletic treatises, minute words of Judaic law, some stories in which the emphasis is upon ethical standards of an earlier culture, which should be passed by in building worship programs. In contrast to these passages there are triumphant expressions of confidence in a living God in some of the psalms; there are visions of spiritual insight in the utterances of the prophets; there are beautiful accounts of lives made radiant by a sense of companionship with God; there are records of decisions that have changed the life of the world and there are inspired words ringing with an authoritative reality which came out of the tested experience of Jesus of Nazareth.

Since the Bible reveals to us how men have grown in the adequacy of their concepts of God, we shall choose for worship those selections which give us worthy concepts of God. Some of our older hymnals contain in their responsive services sections of some of the imprecatory psalms in which the ideas of God are entirely contrary to our Christian teachings.[7] These sections represent Hebrew religious experience at its lowest, the natural outcome of the civilization of the times, but not the expression of their great prophets.

Scripture passages will help to achieve the aims of worship in so far as they relate to the life-experiences of those who are worshiping. Doctor Soares reminds us that all history, including the Bible, began in experience. The biblical material was once vivid, living experience, and it is this "experience quality" which we want to recapture for modern worship. We shall need to remem-

---

[7] Some denominations have been revising their responsive services so that they may express the religious convictions and aspirations of the present day.

ber that while there are certain universal experiences which are common to all generations, it may not be possible to find a selection from the Bible which applies specifically to every present-day problem, and we do not want to inhibit the mood of worship by using biblical material which, only by much twisting of its original meaning, can be made to apply to the present need.

We shall need to be careful that the Scripture is adapted to the understanding of the age group. Insincerity and unreality in the religious life may result from saying with our lips in worship material which has no meaning for us.

The Use of Biblical Material in Worship. There are two or three outstanding needs which confront us in deciding how to use the Scriptures in worship. One of these is the need to make the biblical material vivid and compelling to the attention of the worshiper. When familiar or partly familiar passages are introduced with no attempt to make them meaningful, the well-known words, however beautiful, often fall upon unlistening ears. We need to study new approaches to make these rather familiar passages live again, so that we may listen to them with that freshness of interest which attaches itself to something new. For this reason, it is often helpful to preface the reading of Scripture with some statement or some narrative material to make its meaning more vivid.

Let us imagine that selections from the Sermon on the Mount are to be read in the worship service. Before the reading the leader holds up a copy of Burnand's picture, "And the Common People Heard Him Gladly." In this picture we do not see Jesus. Instead we look into the anxious, eager faces of the crowd who are listening to him. Their eyes are fastened hungrily upon him, and we feel, though we do not see, his presence. The leader may say to the group: "What do you imagine that he is saying to make these anxious, care-laden faces appear so tense with excitement? Will you watch their faces and listen to his voice as I read his words?" Then, will follow the reading of the Scripture.

A college group caught a new significance in the story of the calling of the disciples after a dramatic dialogue between James and John and their father Zebedee, in which the two sons try to make their father understand why they felt that they want to follow Jesus.

The association of these passages with pictures is one method of approach. Sometimes a vivid retelling of the story may include the reading of part of the material from the Bible itself.

If Scripture passages are to be vital sources for worship, appreciation of their content must precede participation in worship. The worship values in them must be clearly discerned and felt. They must glow with interest and reality. If it is story material, the pictures must stand out vividly, the characters really live. In the case of other passages the worshiper is often helped by an appreciation of the living experience out of which the passage came. This kindling of appreciation can often be done in a period of preparation for worship,[8] or it may become a part of the worship experience itself.

Methods of Using Biblical Material. There are various methods of using biblical material in worship. It may be read by the leader, or in a young people's service by one of the young people. It may be read responsively. It may be read in unison, or it may be repeated in uni-

---

[8] See Chap. X, "Preparation for Worship."

son from memory. If it is read by one person for the group, the reader ought to read well, so that the selection has real meaning for the group. Since we seek participation in worship by the whole group, unison reading or recitation would seem to provide this opportunity better than any other method. For little children who cannot handle mimeographed sheets or Bibles easily, the memorization of Scripture has its advantages, though there are times when second and third-year children may read a short selection from the blackboard or from a children's Bible.

As children grow older and pass into the Junior Department, it is not always possible to memorize sufficient worship material to enrich the worship service. If we limited our use of worship materials to just such selections as the children have memorized, we should impoverish some of our services of worship as well as the experience of the children. It is possible for these boys and girls to read Scripture from a mimeographed copy, and enjoy its meaning, if they have first studied it in a previous period of preparation. If they read Scripture from their Bibles it is essential that all have the same translation.

Shall we prefer responsive or unison readings? Let us remind ourselves that in many responsive readings the thought is interrupted by the division into sections. Responsive readings are of greater significance when they were originally written to be used antiphonally. Then the thought falls into natural divisions.

With children, in responsive services, what is apt to happen is that the child participates while *he is reading,* but his attention and interest wander while the leader reads. For this reason unison reading provides far more vital means of participation in worship for the child, unless the selection is antiphonal in its very nature, as Psalm 24, and the boys and girls know the story of it, and how it was used in the Temple service. If this is so, they will enter into it eagerly, each part of the group listening to the other and ready with its response.

LITERATURE AS A SOURCE OF WORSHIP MATERIAL

Worship may be greatly enriched by the use of selections from the world's literature. Men and women since the days of the Bible have held communion with God and have expressed in beautiful literary form the new visions of God which that communion has brought to them.

Poetry in Worship. Because the poets have caught the vision of the inner meanings of life and have been able to put these inner meanings in forms of beauty which make them unforgettable, there is much poetry which will enrich the worship experience.

Not all age groups and not all individuals appreciate and enjoy poetry to an equal degree. But a love of the world's greatest poetry is one means of building a beautiful character and we may well use periods of preparation to stimulate an enjoyment of poems which will help us to live more truly religious lives and which we can use as a language of worship.

For adolescents almost the whole field of poetical literature holds possibilities of enjoyment. For children the selection is more limited, but they will respond to the following types of poems: Poems of action, story poems, concrete and vivid nature poems, poems referring to such special days as Christmas, poems with a slogan, poems about any familiar experience. Adolescents too will enjoy many of the above, with the added possibility of those containing more abstract truth.

All of our poetry, of course, will be selected to make more vivid or concrete the theme of worship. The following poems illustrate the possibility of finding selections appropriate for certain themes:

Joy in Work: "Work," by Henry van Dyke.

Joy in the Out of Doors: "A Chant Out of Doors," by Marguerite Wilkinson.

Overcoming Handicaps — Meeting Life Bravely: "How Did You Die?" by Edward Vance Cooke.

Gratitude for Out of Doors: "For Flowers That Bloom," by Ralph Waldo Emerson.

Poems for worship should not be too long, and they are of special helpfulness when the whole group recites them together. Sometimes the full meaning of a poem is hard to get, even by older groups, when it is heard read by another person for the first time. When boys and girls actually see the words, they are better able to visualize the meaning.

Poetry, to be used with value, must be understood. Appreciation periods in which poems to be used in worship are read and discussed will greatly enhance the enjoyment which the group may have in them as well as their significance in the worship services.

If poetry is read by one person it should be read well, for poetry is rhythmical and requires a fine feeling of appreciation not only of its meaning but of its sound.

And, last of all, we should be careful not to overload our worship services with poetry. A group of adolescent boys were sitting in criticism upon some of the worship services in their department. "Too much poetry," said one of the boys. "Those girls are always bringing in this poetry stuff."

Prose Selections for Worship. In addition to poetry there are inspiring prose selections which may be used to enrich services of worship. One of the great satisfactions which comes to those who are planning a worship curriculum is the enrichment of their own devotional life through becoming familiar with the Bible and the world's other great religious literature.

Our religious life may be deepened and our spiritual horizons broadened by the use of some of the fine devotional materials of other faiths and races than our own. If it is true that

> "Wherever man cries out to God
> The living God is there,"

our own worship can be considerably enriched by the expressions of other religious groups in their search for the living God.[9]

There is a crying need for more worship materials which contain a message for the present day. There are available a few collections of such materials, but we have need of more contributions of this kind. We need litanies, responsive services, and prose selections which voice the social needs of the present century and which express the aspirations of the day in which we live.[10] Here is an opportunity for creative artists who understand the theory and practice of worship and who have the gift of literary expression.

There have been some interesting attempts to experiment with new forms and materials of worship.[11]   Only

---

[9] See *Treasure House of the Living Religions*, by R. E. Hume. Charles Scribner's Sons.
[10] As, *Living Creatively*, by Kirby Page.
[11] See "Additional Reading Sources," at close of this chapter.

as leaders are interested to study the needs and interests of groups who are worshiping in widely different situations, only as they try to interpret and express through the materials of worship the newly emerging aspirations of the present day, can worship be kept vital and invigorating and be not merely form but experience itself.

ADDITIONAL READING SOURCES

Dearmer, Percy, and Others, *The Necessity of Art*. The Morehouse Publishing Co.

Fiske, Walter, *The Recovery of Worship*. The Macmillan Company.

Vogt, Von Ogden, *Modern Worship*. Yale University Press.

Books Containing Worship Materials

Beacon Press. *Responsive Readings*.

Brown, William Adams, *The Quiet Hour*. Association Press.

Burkhart, Roy A., *Seeking the Living Way*. The Abingdon Press, New York.

Chadwick, Samuel, *The Path of Prayer*. The Abingdon Press, New York.

Coit, Stanton, *Social Worship*. Macmillan Co., London.

Cushman, Bishop Ralph S., *Spiritual Hilltops*. The Abingdon Press, New York.

Girl's Every Day Book. Woman's Press.

Holmes, John Haynes, *Readings From Great Authors*. Dodd, Mead & Co.

Hume, R. E., *Treasure House of the Living Religions*. Charles Scribner's Sons.

Hoyland, J. S., *The Sacrament of Common Life*. W. Heffer & Sons, Ltd., Cambridge, England.

Leavens, Robert F., *Great Companions*. The Beacon Press.

Mattoon, L. I., and Bragdon, H. D., *Services for the Open*. D. Appleton-Century Company.

Page, Kirby, *Living Creatively*. Farrar and Rinehart.

Weatherhead, Leslie D., *Discipleship*. The Abingdon Press, New York.

Williams, Griswold, *Antiphonal Readings for Free Worship*. The Beacon Press.

Woman's Press, *A Book of Services for Group Worship*.

Collections of Stories

Anonymous, *By An Unknown Disciple*. Doran.

Bailey, Temple, *The Holly Hedge*. Penn Publishing Company.

Berg, Mary K., *Story Worship Services for the Junior Church*, Chap. V. Harper & Brothers.

Boeckel, Florence B., *Through the Gateway*, Vol. I, of Books of Goodwill. National Council for Prevention of War.

Bonser, Edna Madison, *How the Early Hebrews Lived and Learned*. The Macmillan Company.

Bonser, Edna Madison, *The Little Boy of Nazareth*. Harper & Brothers.

Cather, Katherine Dunlap, *Educating By Story Telling*. World Book Company.

Crownfield, Gertrude, *The Feast of Noel*. E. P. Dutton & Co.

Center, Stella Stewart, *The Worker and His Work*. J. B. Lippincott Company.

Condon, Randall J., *The Atlantic Readers*. Little, Brown & Company.

Egan, Joseph B., *Character Training Through Story, Study, Work, and Play*. Welles Publishing Company.

Gibran, Kahlil, *Jesus, the Son of Man*. Alfred G. Knopf.

Lyman, Rollo, and Hill, Howard C., *Literature and Living*, Books I, II, and III. Charles Scribner's Sons.

May, William J., *Living Bible Stories*. The Abingdon Press.

May, William J., *Bible Stories and How to Tell Them*. Cokesbury Press.

Niebuhr, Hulda, *Greatness Passing By*. Charles Scribner's Sons.

Payson, Anne Byrd, *I Follow the Road*. The Abingdon Press.

Sharp, Dallas Lore, *Romances From the Old Testament*. The Abingdon Press.

Sherman, Henry A., and Kent, Charles Foster, *The Children's Bible*. Charles Scribner's Sons.

Starbuck, E. D., and Shuttleworth, Frank K., *Guide to Books for Character Training*. The Macmillan Company.

Van Buren, Maud, and Bemis, Katherine, *Christmas in Storyland*. The Macmillan Company. *Christmas in Modern Story*. D. Appleton-Century Co.

Biography

Cottler, Joseph, and Jaffe, Haym, *Heroes of Civilization*. Little, Brown & Company.

De Kruif, Paul Henry, *Microbe Hunters* and *Hunger Fighters*. Harcourt, Brace and Company.

Kirkland, Winifred, *Portrait of a Carpenter*. Charles Scribner's Sons.

Kirkland, Winifred and Frances, *Girls Who Made Good*. Harper & Brothers.

Logie, Iona M. R. (Ed.), *Careers in the Making*. Harper & Brothers. (Readings in recent biography as a means of vocational guidance.)

Lansing, Marion F., *Great Moments in Freedom*. Doubleday, Doran and Company.

Wade, Mary H., *The Wonder Workers*. Little, Brown & Company.

Wallace, Archer, *Overcoming Handicaps*. Harper & Brothers.

Wildman, Edwin, *Famous Leaders of Character*. L. C. Page.

Poetry

A. For Adolescents and Adults

Auslander, Joseph, and Hill, *The Winged Horse Anthology*. Doubleday, Doran and Company.

Clark, Thomas Curtis, *Quotable Poems*, Vols. I and II. Willett, Clark, and Colby.

Clark, Thomas Curtis, *Poems for Special Days and Occasions*. Harper & Brothers.

Clark, Thomas Curtis, *Poems of Justice*. Willett, Clark, and Colby.

Oxenham, John, *"Gentlemen, the King!"* The Pilgrim Press.

Oxenham, John, *The Te Deums and the Sacraments*. The Pilgrim Press.

Slack, Elvira, *Christ in the Poetry of To-day*. Woman's Press.

Hill, Caroline M., *The World's Great Religious Poetry*. The Macmillan Company.

Mearns, Hughes, *Creative Power and Creative Youth*. Doubleday, Doran and Company.

Mountsier, Mabel, *Singing Youth*. Harper & Brothers.

Merrifield, Fred, *Modern Religious Verse and Prose*. Charles Scribner's Sons.

Sergent, Nellie B., *Younger Poets*. An Anthology of American Secondary School Verse. D. Appleton-Century Company.

Shipman, Dorothy M., *Stardust and Holly* (an excellent anthology of Christmas poems). The Macmillan Company.

B. For Children

Barrows, Marjorie, *One Hundred Best Poems for Boys and Girls*. Whitman Publishing Company.

Mountsier, Mabel, *Singing Youth*. Harper & Brothers.

Stevenson, Burton E. and Elizabeth B., *Days and Deeds*. Doubleday, Doran and Company.

Thompson, Blanche J., *Silver Pennies*. The Macmillan Company.

Untermeyer, Louis, *This Singing World*. Harcourt, Brace and Company.

Interesting Creative Experiments in Worship Materials

Cross, Earle Bennett, *Modern Worship and the Psalter*. The Macmillan Company.

Harris, Thomas L., *Christian Public Worship*. (Contains three forms for the sacrament of communion; also experiments with services of silence.) Harper & Brothers.

Guthrie, Norman, *Offices of Mystical Religion*. D. Appleton-Century Company.

Religious Education

International Journal of Religious Education, May, 1933, "A Ritual in Rhythm," by Nancy Longenecker.

Talks

Cheley, F. H., *Stories for Talks to Boys*. Association Press.

Fiske, Walter, *In a College Chapel*. Harper & Brothers.

Stocking, Jay, *The Child in the Congregation*. The Pilgrim Press.

Weston, Sidney (Ed.), *Sermons I Have Preached to Young People*. The Pilgrim Press.

CHAPTER VII

VISUALIZATION MATERIALS IN WORSHIP

Man will respond (to the Vision of God) by imagination.
His expression of the Vision will take shape in things that are
the products of his hand's cunning. He will make temples, and
paintings and sculpture. . . .

Man instinctively responds to God by ritual. He is dramatic in his religious self-expression. He breaks out into
cheers and pæans and psalms. . . .

It is worth remembering that the Christian idea of God is
itself imagined in the form of a great Drama. A divine action
on the human stage shows us what God is and what he has
done for us.—A. S. DUNCAN-JONES.

From *The Necessity of Art,* by Dearmer and Others. Pp. 79, 81,
98.

"ONE can live without art, but not so well," someone
has said. We might alter the wording a little and find it
equally true that one can *worship* without art, but not
so well. This is as true of boys and girls as of adults,
and as true to-day as when the great cathedrals and
chapels of the Old World were being fashioned.

Within the last generation a change has taken place
in our thinking about art. In the nineteenth century
the cry, "Art for art's sake," was the slogan of those who
sought beauty. To-day we hear a great art critic say,
"The object of art is not to give pleasure, as our fathers
assumed, but to express the highest spiritual realities."[1]

We have already seen[2] the close relationship which
exists between the appreciation of beauty and the religious feelings. The religious experience of beauty

[1] Percy Dearmer, *The Necessity of Art,* Preface, p. v. Student
Christian Movement.
[2] Chap. II, "Aids to Worship."

stimulates in us "strange new impulses."[3] For this reason art has ever been the handmaiden of religion. We need not be afraid of the religious experience of beauty. Much of our so-called religion has been painfully lacking in beauty and charm. Goodness should allure because of its beauty and the experience of worship should be throughout an experience of joy.

Art not only ministers to us through the moral uses of beauty, but also visualizes the religious experience. The processes of recollection and contemplation, which are parts of the worship experience, need stimulating in some vivid way. We have seen the power of the story to do this;[4] a picture is a story on canvas; pieces of sculpture may be "sermons in stone," and a religious drama may become an enactment of the presence of God.

PICTURES AS WORSHIP MATERIALS

Pictures are the most easily accessible form of art for use in the worship services of most church schools. Fortunately, it is possible to-day to secure an increasing number of reproductions of great pictures at reasonable prices, so that art is brought within the reach of all of us. Since pictures represent art in one of its most definitely concrete forms, they have special value for making truths vivid.

Selecting Pictures for Worship. We are not limited in our selection of pictures for worship to those on so-called *religious* subjects. Some of those not treating at all of biblical themes will have a real religious significance. Who shall say which will be more helpful in the worship experience of a six-year-old, Sir Joshua Reyn-

---

[3] H. N. Wieman, *Methods of Private Religious Living*, p. 132. The Macmillan Company.
[4] Chap. VI, "Materials of Worship."

olds' "The Infant Samuel," or Millet's "Feeding Her
Birds"? And, surely, there is no irreverence in linking
"Washington at Prayer in Valley Forge" with Hof-
mann's "Jesus in Gethsemane," or Ferris' "Lincoln the
Railsplitter" with a picture of Jesus in the Carpenter
Shop.

Sometimes pictures which are not religious in the
sense that their themes are specifically "religious," may
be interpreted in such a way that they meet a worship
need. Albright's "At the End of the Pier," Roos's "The
Hoople Race," or Israel's "Children of the Sea," if they
help a child to remember all the happiness he has had
in play so that he wants to thank God for it, are truly
worship pictures.

The adolescent may worship through such pictures as
"Her Son," by Nellie V. L. Walker; "The Boy and the
Angel," by Thayer; and Alexander's "Boy of Winander," if he feels that the light in the eyes of the
adolescent boys in all three pictures indicates that each

> ". . . by the vision splendid
> Is on his way attended."

A group of adults in a fishing village may be led to
see a religious significance in their own labor through a
picture of their own fishermen struggling with the sea
if it is associated in their thinking with a picture of
"Jesus and the Fishermen."

The leader of worship will have to study the picture-
interests of his group, to be sure that the picture is one
which the worshiper will enjoy. Appreciation is an intimately personal experience. No one can appreciate
for another person. And if we do not enjoy a work of
art, it has no great message for us.

We shall remember not to offer children pictures with symbolical meanings, since they are literalists and require story pictures. Just as the story rather than the allegory must carry the message to children at least up to the age of ten, so the story picture rather than the allegorical one will kindle their appreciation.

With adolescence comes that quickening sensitiveness to the inner meanings of things. The adolescent can understand Holman Hunt's "The Light of the World," or Cornicelius' "Christ Tempted by Satan," when the symbolism of these pictures would be only baffling to a younger child. The former picture is often seen on the walls of Junior rooms, when a less symbolic picture such as Hofmann's "Head of Jesus," or Copping's "The Sermon on the Mount," would speak a more direct message.

The younger we are the more we respond to pictures which are full of action and which tell their own story. For children either Hofmann's or Clemens' picture of "The Rich Young Ruler" tells the story in a direct way. Not until adolescence or adult years are they able to enter completely into the mood of Watts's "For He Had Great Possessions," though all these pictures portray the same incident.

In our selection of worship pictures we want to make sure that the picture does not convey a wrong or unpleasant idea of God. Many of the earliest concepts of children can be traced back to the pictures which they have seen. We do not want any pictures to interfere with the beauty and joy of worship. The pictures we look at should have the effect of drawing us near to God.

Pictures of Jesus will be important too, for Jesus is the embodiment to us of all that radiant religious living should be. Many pictures of Jesus painted by modern artists are more satisfactory and pleasing for boys and girls and young people than those painted by the old masters. Such artists as William Hole, Harold Copping, and Siemeradski have given us a pleasing Jesus, not against a background of Italian landscape or Flemish village life, but in the natural Palestine setting where Jesus actually lived.

As a rule, pictures in color have a greater appeal than those in sepia or in black and white. They have this advantage, that if the original is a painting, we get more of the real atmosphere of the original from a reproduction in color. Fortunately, it is becoming increasingly easy to get good colored reproductions of great paintings at reasonable prices. However, adults who have seen the originals of paintings can by association enjoy a sepia print, and it is often possible to get sepia copies when colored ones are unavailable. And it is also true that though we think of children as preferring color, many of the charming books for boys and girls to-day are illustrated in black and white, and one editor of children's books says that there is no reason why children cannot learn to enjoy black-and-white illustrations if they are good ones. For any age group a good sepia reproduction is far better than a crudely colored one.

The picture for use in worship with large groups must be large enough to enable the entire group to see it and appreciate its details. Some pictures do not have carrying value; they may be too dark or too indistinct to be used in group work.

Types of Pictures for Worship. First of all, there will be the picture which suggests the attitude of worship.

And what is the worship attitude? Is it not made up of a combination of several attitudes? Pictures of this type may express gratitude, reverence, wonder, joy, dedication, and other great emotions. In some way they suggest the need of God and of his presence. In the following list, which illustrates this type of picture, some are listed as for children and some for older groups, but these lists are not mutually exclusive. "Religion," by Pearce, is listed as an adult interest, but a group of primary children have been known to worship through it most satisfactorily because their background had been enriched by stories of the ways in which people worshiped in the early Old-Testament days. Similarly, "The Angelus" has a universal appeal for all ages, as have many of the other pictures.

Children

"The Infant Samuel," Reynolds.
"Now I Lay Me Down to Sleep," Smith.
"The Day's Beginning in Washington's Home," Ferris.

Adolescents

"The Vigil," Pettie.
"The Oath of Knighthood," Abbey.
"Behold, I Send You Forth," Tarrant.
"Christ Among the Doctors," Hofmann.
"The Boy of Winander," Alexander.
"Thy Kingdom Come," Larsen.[5]

Adults and All Ages

"Pilgrims Going to Church," Boughton.
"The Song of the Lark," Breton.
"The Angelus," Millet.
"The Appeal to the Great Spirit," Dallin.
"When I Consider Thy Heavens," Taylor.
"When I Meditate Upon Thee in the Night Watches," Taylor.
"Christ Blessing the Meal," Von Uhde.
"Christ Among the Lowly," L'Hermitte.

[5] May be purchased through B. A. McGarvey, 143 Ross Street, Williamsport, Pennsylvania.

VISUALIZATION MATERIALS

Another group of pictures is those which interpret the ideal which the worship service is emphasizing. Here we have a wide variety of choice, and every leader will want to keep a classified list to which he adds a new picture from time to time as he hears of it.

Sometimes we discover that a picture used before with a different significance can be used again to interpret a new ideal, and the picture has for the group the added charm of familiarity. With a new meaning it establishes new associations in the brain, and its message becomes more intimately the possession of the one who enjoys it. Following are a few illustrations of how pictures may help in the visualization of an ideal.

Worship Ideal: Doing Hard Things
  "The Young Pioneer," Volk.
  "The Boy Lincoln," Eastman Johnson.
  "Pilgrims Going to Church," Boughton.
  "The Old Santa Fe Trail," Younghunter.
  "The Rail Splitter," Ferris.
  "Washington Crossing the Delaware," Leutze.
  "The Embarkation of the Pilgrims," Weir.

Worship Ideal: Our Homes and Families
  "The Day's Beginning in Washington's Home," Ferris.
  "Home Keeping Hearts Are Happiest," Taylor.
  "Madame Le Brun and Her Daughter," Le Brun.
  "The Last Ray," Breton.
  "Christ Among the Lowly," L'Hermitte.
  "The Children's Hour," Taylor.
  "Detail From the Holy Night," Correggio.
  "Grandmother's Story," Merle.

Worship Ideal: Dedication
  "The Vigil," Pettie.
  "Sir Galahad," Keyser.
  "The Oath of Knighthood," Abbey.
  "Penn's Vision," Oakley.
  "Penn's Treaty With the Indians," Abbey.

"Lincoln at Gettysburg," Oakley.
"The Knight of the Holy Grail," Waugh.

Another significant application of pictures to worship is their use in taking the everyday experiences of life and raising them to the level of worship. To make life worth living we must have the feeling that God cares, that we are serving him and living the God-life in all of the everyday relationships of play, study, work, and family ties. In the worship service on Sunday we may catch up all of these everyday activities into a feeling that they are infinitely worth while because God is in them all. And so we go back to them with a new dedication, to enjoy them and to be a child of God in them. Some of the pictures which we might select to reveal the religious meaning in these everyday experiences will not suggest God to the pupil unless through study and interpretation of them we help him to see that meaning in them. But if such pictures suggest the dignity of labor, the beauty of home life, the presence of God in nature, gratitude for work, the opportunities of wholesome play, and the desirability of Christlike friendliness, we may use them to reveal how all of these situations are stepping-stones to God. In the following list no attempt is made to indicate which pictures apply to any one of these specific possibilities just mentioned, but a study of the titles will make their application sufficiently clear.

"Labor," Pearce.
"Recreation," Pearce.
"The Voice of the Falls," Couse.
"The Angelus," Millet.
"De Profundis," Mosher.
"The Rail Splitter," Ferris.
"Washington, the American Cincinnatus," Ferris.

"Motherly Care," Israels.
"Christ in a School in Brittany," Von Uhde.
"Christ Among the Lowly," L'Hermitte.
"Little Sister," Israels.
"Her Son," Walker.

There is, of course, always the possibility of using pictures to celebrate the religious meaning of such special days as Christmas, Thanksgiving, patriotic days, and other great home, national, or church festivals. The important thing is that we shall search for pictures which the group will *enjoy* and that we shall try to find pictures new as well as old, so that fresh meaning may be suggested.

Often it is helpful to show more than one artist's interpretation of a subject. This allows for individual differences in taste. It stimulates the imagination, also, to compare several possible interpretations. Perhaps the most familiar of all the pictures of the boy Jesus is Hofmann's "Christ Among the Doctors." This story of the youthful Jesus might take on new meanings if the Hofmann picture were compared with Hunt's "The Finding of Christ in the Temple," Leinweber's "Jesus in the Temple" and a photograph of a sculptured relief done by a recent artist, John Angel.

In the attempt to visualize the boy Jesus and make him a real personality, a group of boys and girls might be interested to collect as many pictures of his youth as possible, discussing the likable qualities which each artist has portrayed. Following are some pictures of the youthful Jesus:

Millais, "Jesus in the Home of His Parents."
Murillo, "The Boy Jesus."
Dagnan-Bouveret, "The Child Jesus."
Murillo, "Joseph and the Child Jesus."

Donatello, "The Christ Child and Saint John."
Herbert, "The Youth of Our Lord."
Angel, "Christ Among the Doctors."[6]
Hofmann, "Christ Among the Doctors."
Hunt, "The Finding of Christ in the Temple."

How to Use Pictures in Worship. There naturally arises the question of how best to use pictures in worship. Many of our church schools are recognizing the need not only of a worship period, but also of a period devoted to preparation for worship.[7] Sometimes the interpretation of pictures comes better in this preliminary period than in the worship service itself. The leader will have to determine which is the better procedure with each service in mind and its aims and objectives.

One of the best ways to make a picture live for boys and girls is by using it in an appreciation lesson. By informal conversation and exchange of ideas they share in discovering its meaning. Sometimes this can best be done in a preparatory period, though in informal worship periods the interpretation of a picture often stimulates an immediate worship response.

Worship pictures may be hung where all may look at them even though no specific reference is made to them. Certainly, after a worship picture has been studied for its meaning, it may hang before the group for more than one Sunday so that by recall the significance of the picture may give meaning to future worship experiences.

As to the technique of using pictures, let us remember that in studying a picture the enjoyment of it may be ruined by too minute questioning. A classroom period

[6] A reproduction can be secured from the artist, Mr. John Angel, 149 East 119th Street, New York City.
[7] See Chap. X, "Preparation for Worship."

which suggests to the group that we are trying to make them like the picture, or that we want to drag out of them expressions of feeling which they do *not* feel, will give them an actual distaste for it. An appreciation lesson is an "enjoyment" lesson above everything else. The leader must first of all enjoy the picture himself. Then he must understand how to suggest enjoyment to others without dogmatically telling them that they should enjoy it because he does. Occasionally some young person may not enjoy a picture as we do. He has a right to his own preference.

Sometimes the story of the artist or a story about the picture itself, how it came to be painted or what it has meant to someone else, will enhance the power of its message. But this is not inevitably so. Merely to know the details of an artist's life does not insure appreciation of one of his pictures. If the facts about an artist help to interpret the picture and enhance its significance, then they will prove stimulating worship material. To know the facts about the birth and education of the modern artist Beneker may be quite uninteresting. But if, in studying his picture, "Men Are Square," the group learns that workingmen have always had a fascination for him; if they imagine him, as a boy, gazing into the fiery furnaces of a steel foundry, or watching the men way up on the scaffoldings of high buildings; if they begin to feel with him that work is splendid and that workmen *are* square, then the picture may help them to worship in a service whose aim is to help us feel our fellowship with the workers of the world.

Often a picture and its interpretation may be the means of stimulating a worship activity which will have a continuing influence in life outside of the group. In a small school the college chapel services for several weeks centered in the study of Burnand's picture, "Saint's Saturday." This picture portrays the disciples in an upper room the day after the crucifixion. One of the disciples is seated at one end of the table, with his head bowed in his hands in an attitude of utter despair and loss. The others are grouped about him, some seated, some standing. Their faces express various moods of bewilderment, sorrow, puzzled questioning, and futility. There is no key as to which disciple is which in the picture.

In the opening chapel service the picture hung over the altar where all could see it. The service included a dialogue between Peter and Andrew, just after Peter had denied Jesus. The young man who took the part of Peter portrayed this repentant disciple with masterly force. The following hymn was sung:

"Holy, holy, holy, Lord, thy disciples
    Gather in devotion to sing and dream of thee;
Holy, holy, holy, beautiful and gracious,
    Still in our hearts we dwell in Galilee.

"Holy, holy, holy, still in the morning
    Mending our fishernets, we hail thee by the shore;
Friend, Guide and Brother, by the wells of evening
    Deep from thy voice we drink thy healing lore.

"Holy, holy, holy, Lord, thy disciples
    Ever through the ages live again because of thee;
Holy, holy, holy, all thy ways we follow,
    From Bethlehem to dark Gethsemane."[3]

Then booklets were distributed containing the names of all the disciples and the biblical references to each one. The members of the group were asked to read

---

[3] Percy MacKaye. Found in *The American Student Hymnal*. D. Appleton-Century Company. Used by permission of the author.

these references during the week and to study the picture, trying to determine which character in the picture represented each disciple.

The chapel service the following week took the form of informal conversation as individuals told how they interpreted the characters. The effort was made to feel the reality of these friends of Jesus and through a study of them to feel the reality of his personality.

The Use of the Stereopticon in Worship. Some churches have experimented with the use of the stereopticon in worship, and when this is carefully planned and well done, a worshipful experience can be stimulated. To be effective, however, this does require careful planning. The operator of the machine must change the slides at exactly the right moment; there must be no mistakes or delays. If pictures are used, the slides must be artistically colored. Words of hymns must be clear so all can read them. The organist or pianist must have a complete outline of the service with the places where music is to come in plainly indicated. If a beautiful picture of a worshipful character is on the screen as the congregation assembles, and if soft music is playing, this will help to obviate any consciousness of the mechanism of the screen or the machine.

Few churches as yet are equipped with moving-picture and talking machines, and one cannot safely prophesy how much the church of the future will make use of such equipment. As yet there have been few moving pictures produced with messages so spiritually dynamic that they offer material for worship. One can imagine that if such great religious messages should be as effectively produced as a few of the finest talking pictures have been, and if such productions were available for use by churches, the results might be tremendous. Most of the moving pictures to date which have attempted to portray religious themes have suffered from the defects of oversensationalism or uncritical biblical scholarship or plain mediocrity. There have been a few recent moving pictures, not directly religious, which have had stirring messages, but most of these are not available for church use, owing to the expense involved and the lack of equipment.

The possible combination of visual and auditory images to stimulate worship attitudes offers a field for experimentation. There have been some very interesting attempts to do this thing by synchronizing music with stereopticon pictures.[9] In such a worship service the room may be in semidarkness as the worshipers arrive. Soft music is playing (this may be Victrola records or selections by a musician) and on the screen a shadow cross against a blue blackground or a picture which sets the theme for the service of worship. The service moves along with the call to worship or Scripture read by a leader, hymns and responses for the congregation thrown upon the screen, and a succession of pictures whose message is interpreted by appropriate music. This type of worship service can be both very artistic and very worshipful, and there is a real opportunity for creative leadership in such experiments.

DRAMATIZATION IN WORSHIP

In recent years there has been a revival of interest in the religious uses of the drama. In many situations it has been applied with great effectiveness as one process of education with children, young people, and adults.

[9] See H. Paul Janes, *Screen and Projector in Christian Education.*

Under different circumstances and with other leadership it has apparently failed to do all that its enthusiastic advocates claim for it. The effectiveness of a method, of course, should be tested by that method at its best and not by its failures, but there is evidently need to re-examine our first enthusiasm and attempt to discover just what results drama may be expected to produce and use it for those ends.

We are concerned here with the place of dramatic material *in worship*. One who would feel the possibilities of dramatizing the worship experience should steep himself in the accounts of how drama was used in the early days of the church to lead the people Godward. Then he should compare the customs, religious attitudes, and worship settings of those bygone days with our present religious and community customs and attitudes.[10]

Opportunities for Uses of Drama in Worship. Drama may help to visualize the ideals of worship. "The Servant in the House" makes vivid the possibility of re-living the Christ life in modern life. The miracle play, "Everyman," visualizes the search of the human soul for God. *The Rock*[11] unfolds before the worshiper the transformation of a vacillating man into the dependability and strength which are God's.

As these great dramas unfold before our eyes, we live vicariously through the experience of the drama. We ourselves are living it, not merely watching others live. So we identify ourselves with the life of God. When

[10] Brander Matthews, *The Development of the Drama*. Charles Scribner's Sons.
    K. L. Bates, *The English Religious Drama*. The Macmillan Company.
    Helen L. Willcox, *Bible Study Through Educational Dramatics*.
[11] By Mary P. Hamlin. The Pilgrim Press.

religious drama is well done, it stirs the emotions, it arouses new impulses, and it may have the effect of giving us new faith in the possibilities of Christlike living.

It is evident that dramatization often has its chief values in its influence upon the participants rather than upon the audience. Of course this is assuming that the dramatization has proceeded upon an educational basis and has not been the mere memorizing of parts in order to put on a "show performance" or "to keep the young people interested," or to "draw crowds to the minister's evening service." For those who are actively participating, the vicarious experience often becomes very real.

For those who work with children it is well to consider how much use of dramatic material we shall make *in worship,* when the goal of worship is to afford opportunity for the expression of communion with God to the *entire* worshiping group. Do we want only a small group (those dramatizing) to worship or do we covet expression from the whole group? Dramatization certainly has its place in the educational scheme, but perhaps not so large a place as we have supposed in the worship service. Perhaps the real worship experience will take place *in the small group* during the preparation of the dramatization.

Difficulties of the Use of Drama in Worship. There are some obvious difficulties in the incorporation of drama into the service of worship. There is the difficulty presented by mediocre acting and amateurish stage effects which fail to produce a sense of reality. To be sure, the actors, themselves, often will not be conscious of the crudities, but so long as we have one group acting and another group observing there is bound to be some expression of the critical tendency. Let us remember that even our boys and girls to-day are more or less critics of the theater. Constant attendance at moving pictures has produced in them a craving for emotional satisfaction in their drama. While many moving pictures appear to the dramatically educated adult as being woefully inferior in great dramatic power, still there is a dramatic technique united with a perfection of stagecraft which is apt to make cruder effects and simple productions unsatisfactory to the sophisticated young person of to-day.

Now, it is possible to produce very beautiful effects through very simple media, but when the *effect is not produced,* the continuity of the worship experience is interrupted.

Sometimes the youthful participants are self-conscious. Sometimes biblical customs and costumes seem amusing to the observers. Sometimes they are concerned with the "queerness" of certain scenes in foreign countries. It is an interesting fact that while the moving picture brings all the world to their doors, when their friends attempt to do this, they feel an element of strangeness.

It is obvious that when the actors are hesitating or self-conscious, when the electric star in the pageant fails to shine at the right moment, when "Abraham" loses his beard in the midst of a dramatic scene with "Isaac," there is bound to be a resulting loss of reverence, and the harmony of worship is jarred.

However, there are churches which, under the leadership of someone who understands dramatic art but who also understands how to lead the participants to forget themselves in the rendering of a great message, have been able to present religious drama that is sufficiently beautiful and inspiring for worship.

Types of Drama for Worship. Some religious dramatizations will be more valuable for classroom use than for worship. Boys and girls may dramatize some of the Bible stories and perceive new meanings in them. A biblical dramatization may have worth-while educational results and yet not be powerful enough to contribute to the worship experience. We shall choose for worship those dramatizations which will serve a distinct purpose in the *worship life* of the group and whose effect is to arouse in the group a desire to worship.

There is a simple use of dramatization which is effective because it makes no pretense of being "a drama" and because it allows for participation in the dramatization by the whole worshiping group. A Christmas service may be planned during which, as the whole group sings the Christmas hymns and carols, there march in processional down the aisles, Mary, Joseph, the three kings and the shepherds, the group forming a tableau on the altar steps. There is the use of dramatic material read or spoken by the participants, with no attempt at staging or costuming. If this is well done, it is very effective, and the attention of the group is centered in the content rather than in stage accessories.

We are living in a day when education is encouraging the release of the creative instinct and when religious education is experimenting with new forms and contents. So we shall naturally look for creative experiments in the field of worship. We have mentioned such an attempt to synchronize music with the stereopticon. In the field of drama we read of similar experiments. We all know that rhythmic interpretation was part of the primitive religious celebrations. We are not surprised, then, to know that some who are equipped by training to do so are experimenting with a combination of rhythmic descriptive action, poetry and music.[12] This attempt to create a ritual in rhythm must be very artistically done to be effective and must be a sincere effort to express deep religious emotions. Although not many churches may be able to make use of this form of dramatic interpretation in worship, yet it ought not to be overlooked as one of the possibilities which may be further developed in the future.

Methods of Using Drama in Worship. If we are to worship through the drama, the worship setting for the dramatizations must be carefully prepared. Sometimes a preliminary explanation makes the group understand that this is a worship service and that there will be no applause but an atmosphere of worship maintained.

Hymns, Scripture, responses will prepare the group for worship. And the dramatization will slip into the service as easily and as naturally as the leader would arise to tell a story. This means that everything must be in readiness; every actor in his place; no awkward waits, but the curtain pulled the instant the service arrives at the moment for the dramatization.

If there must be intervals between the scenes of the drama, the worship feeling should be sustained through those intervals by music, the singing of hymns, or some opportunity for the expression of feeling on the part of the worshipers. After one scene a hymn may be sung,

---

[12] See *International Journal of Religious Education*, May, 1933, article by Nancy Longenecker, "A Ritual in Rhythm," an experimental worship service developed through the correlation of music, poetry, and descriptive action. Stephens College, Missouri, has also experimented with the use of rhythmic expression to induce worship in college chapel services.

after another Scripture read or repeated in unison, and at the close of the drama an opportunity for prayer given.

For the purposes of worship there should be no obtrusive mechanism of stage arrangements. As a rule, the simpler the settings and the fewer changes of scenery, the better.

The participants in a religious drama should feel that they have a message to give to the others. They should, as far as possible, be conscious of this message and its relation to the whole service of worship. The ideal situation exists where this little group enters into its own brief worship service before it presents its message.

NATURE MATERIALS IN WORSHIP

There are times when nature itself, and not its representation in art, may supply the materials for worship.

Objectives in the Use of Nature Material. Here, again, our objectives are those of worship. We will use nature materials to reveal the beauty of God's world, or to make the worshipers feel God's power, the marvels of his planning, or the majesty of his laws.

Types of Nature Materials. There are flowers from the fields, golden rod and asters in the fall of the year, pussy willows and dogwood blossoms in the spring. There are great branches of autumn foliage with their splendor of color. There are the Christmas greens which bring the breath of the deep forests into our winter days. All these remind us that

> "He only is the Maker
>   Of all things near and far;
> He paints the wayside flowers,
>   He lights the evening star."

166

There is the green fern or pot of ivy on the table, or a single rose in a vase. As we look at these living things on a cold winter morning, we sing:

> "All beautiful the march of days,
>   As seasons come and go;
> The Hand that shaped the rose hath wrought
>   The crystal of the snow."

There are seed pods of many kinds which say to us:

> "We plow the fields and scatter
>   The good seed on the land,
> But it is fed and watered
>   By God's almighty hand."

And there are shells, fossils, rocks, pieces of petrified wood which suggest the timeless activity of nature.

Methods of Using Nature Materials. Nature materials may be brought in to the worship services and used there. They may be part of the environment of worship created by the leader or they may be sought for and brought in by the pupils, and thus have a greater value in being *their* contribution to worship.

But bringing nature materials into the worship service is no substitute for taking the group out of doors for worship. Those who share the joy of God's out-of-doors with boys and girls and young people in summer camps will testify to the deeper spiritual sensitiveness of these same young people out in the open. Walking down the hillside after a devotional service under the summer stars a young girl remarked, "Somehow God seems so near out here."

A service of worship on "The Trees, God's Senti-nels"[13] will mean more to us out under the overbranch-

---

[13] See *Services for the Open*, Mattoon and Bragdon. D. Appleton Century Company.

ing trees. The theme, "I Will Lift Up Mine Eyes Unto the Hills,"[14] will have new meaning on the mountainside with

> "Dark lines of hills, a golden sky—
> They seem to meet, so close they lie,
> And ofttimes from the glory bright
> The hills are touched with golden light."[15]

ADDITIONAL READING SOURCES

Drama in Worship

Boyd, C. A., *Worship in Drama*. The Judson Press.

Drama Committee of the Federal Council of Churches, *Religious Drama*, Vols. I and II. D. Appleton-Century Company.

Deseo, Lydia Glover, and Phipps, Hulda M., *Looking at Life Through Drama*. The Abingdon Press. (Problems of race, industry, and international good will, etc., presented through the drama. This problem approach to modern plays might easily result in a deepening worship experience. An excellent bibliography of plays relating to problems of modern life.)

Deseo, Lydia Glover, *Friends of Jesus*. The Abingdon Press.

Division of Plays and Pageants of Methodist Episcopal Church, *Seven Dramatic Services of Worship*.

Eastman, Fred, "Finding God Through Drama," in *Finding God Through the Beautiful*. University of Chicago Press.

Eastman, Fred (Ed.), *Modern Religious Dramas*. Henry Holt and Company.

Eastman, Fred, *Plays of American Life*. Samuel French.

Eastman, Fred, and Wilson, Louis, *Drama in the Church*. Willett, Clark & Co.

Goslin, Omar P., and Alexander, R. C., *Worship Through Drama*. Harper & Brothers.

Wood, W. Carleton, *The Dramatic Method in Religious Education*. The Abingdon Press.

Pictures in Worship

Bailey, Albert E., *The Use of Art in Religious Education*. The Abingdon Press.

Beard, Frederica, *Pictures in Religious Education*. Chap. III,

---

[14] See *Services for the Open*, Mattoon and Bragdon. D. Appleton-Century Company.
[15] *Ibid.*

"Pictures in Relation to Worship." Doubleday, Doran and Company.

Caffin, C. H., *How to Study Pictures*. Doubleday, Doran and Company.

Dearmer, Percy, *Christianity and Art*. Association Press.

Dearmer, Percy, and others, *The Necessity of Art*. Christian Student Movement, London.

Irwin, Grace, *Trail Blazers of American Art*. Harper & Brothers.

Lester, K. M., *Great Pictures and Their Stories*. Mentzer, Bush & Company.

Roberts, M. N., *Stories of the Youth of Artists*. T. Y. Crowell Company.

University of Chicago Press, *Finding God Through the Beautiful*.

Vogt, Von Ogden, *Art and Religion*. Yale University Press.

Picture Books for the Church School Library

Athearn, Walter S. (Ed.), *The Master Library*. Foundation Press, Inc.

Lester, K. M., *Great Pictures and Their Stories*. Mentzer, Bush & Company.

Petersham, Maud and Miska, *The Christ Child*. Doubleday, Doran & Company.

Waterhouse, G., *The Gospel Story of Jesus*. Harper & Brothers. (Illustrations by William Hole.)

Picture Firms

Art Extension Society, Westport, Connecticut. J. L. Hammett Co., Kendall Square, Cambridge, Massachusetts. (Artex Prints.)

F. A. Owen Publishing Company, Dansville, New York. (Instructor Picture Study Series.)

University Prints, 11 Boyd Street, Newton, Massachusetts.

Harold Copping Pictures, Upper Canada Tract Society, 8 and 10 Richmond Street, Toronto, Canada.

George O. Brown & Co., 38 Lovett Street, Beverly, Massachusetts.

Perry Pictures Co., Malden, Massachusetts.

Seeman Prints, Rudof Lesch, Agent, 13 W. 42nd Street, New York City.

J. H. Thurston Company, 50 Bromfield Street, Boston, Massachusetts. (Carries in stock lantern slides from all University

Print negatives and all the 122 pictures in A. E. Bailey's Art Studies in the "Life of Christ.")

Copley Prints, Curtis and Cameron, 221 Columbus Avenue, Boston, Massachusetts.

Palmer Picture Company, 120 Boylston Street, Boston, Massachusetts.

The Prang Company, 118 E. 25th Street, New York City.

Medici Prints, Medici Book and Print Shop, 10 Newbury Street, Boston, Mass.

The Stereopticon

Janes, H. Paul, *Screen and Projector in Christian Education.* Westminster Press.

Bailey Religious Art Stereopticon Slides, rented from the Department of Visual Education, Board of Religious Education, 1720 Chouteau Ave., Saint Louis, Mo.

Nature Material

Baker, Robert, *When the Stars Come Out.* Viking Press.

Brown, Louise, *All Night With the Stars.* Woman's Press.

Hartman, Gertrude, *The World We Live in and How It Came to Be.* The Macmillan Company.

Mattoon, Laura I., and Bragdon, Helen D. (Editors), *Services for the Open.* D. Appleton-Century Company.

Perkins, Jeannette, *And Others Call It God.* Harper & Brothers.

Jeans, Sir James, *The Mysterious Universe* and *The Stars in Their Courses.* The Macmillan Company.

Stevens, Bertha, *Child and the Universe.* John Day Company.

Thomson, J. Arthur, *The Bible of Nature.* Charles Scribner's Sons.

Thomson, J. Arthur, *The Outline of Science.* G. P. Putnam Sons.

CHAPTER VIII

MUSIC IN WORSHIP

"[Faith] comes when music stirs us, and the chords,
   Moving on some grand climax, shake our souls
With influx new that makes new energies."
                              —GEORGE ELIOT.
                        From "A Minor Prophet."

IN "Abt Vogler," Browning, speaking of the wonder of music, says:

"But here is the finger of God, a flash of the will that can,
   Existent behind all laws, that made them and, lo, they are!
And I know not if, save in this, such gift be allowed to man,
   That out of three sounds he frame, not a fourth sound, but
      a star.
Consider it well: each tone of our scale in itself is naught;
   It is everywhere in the world—loud, soft, and all is said:
Give it to me to use! I mix it with two in my thought;
   And there! Ye have heard and seen: consider and bow
      the head."

This is just what we do under the spell of great music—we "bow the head," feeling that here, indeed, "is the finger of God." A recent speaker on the place of music in worship mentions the close association between music and liturgy in the early church, and feels that to-day there is a movement toward the place where "the prayer will sing and the music will pray."

THE RELATION OF MUSIC TO WORSHIP

Just as beauty in forms of art stirs our æsthetic emotions and often kindles a response that is worshipful, so

171

the musician weaves together sounds in forms of beauty, and the result is, as Abt Vogler, the organist, said, "Not a fourth sound, but a star," a star that turns the eyes of our spirits heavenward. Jesus, with his marvelous insight, knew what this relationship between beauty and religion was, when he said, "Worship him in beauty."

The Haunting Power of Music. The music of primitive peoples was decidedly rhythmic in quality. To rhythm was added simple melody. Then, last of all, came that combination of several tones which we call harmony. It is this subtle combination of rhythm, melody, and harmony which gives music its haunting power over us. How often we find ourselves humming an air which we were scarcely conscious that we knew, recapturing its melody from some subconscious depths! Music has power to carry us through the whole gamut of emotions, rendering us sad or gay, plaintively wistful or confident, stormy or peaceful.

Since music is so powerful, it can help us to enter into the greatest experience of all, the experience of God. It can "shake our souls with influx new that makes new energies."

The Need for the Best Music. Since it is so powerful in the release of new energies, we should employ only the greatest music in our cultivation of the life of worship. Great religious experiences demand great music for their expression. One cannot enter the presence of God on the wave of a cheap or catchy tune.

THE DEVELOPMENT OF MUSIC APPRECIATION AS A
MEANS TO WORSHIP

"Do you think the songs in that hymnal are suited to children?" is a question often asked by teachers and superintendents with regard to an exceedingly good hymnal now on the market. This question usually evidences not so much a search for truth as a deepseated doubt as to whether children *can* appreciate music of a high grade of excellence. There has seemed to persist in many church schools a prevailing sentiment that great religious music is in some way "beyond" the enjoyment of average boys and girls.

The experience of the public schools throws some light upon this question for us, for in the public schools of America a very wonderful sense of music appreciation has been built up by introducing the boys and girls to the works of great composers, and a delightful response has been given by the children to this music instruction.

Children *can* and *do* enjoy the very best in art, literature, and music if they are trained in the appreciation of the best. Sometimes we hear leaders say of some cheap-tuned religious song, "But the boys and girls just *love* it." Perhaps they are caught by some catchy melody or rhythm; perhaps they do sing it with gusto, but in all probability they would sing a better song with the same enthusiasm if it were given to them. It is true of anything fine and beautiful, as Tennyson made Guinevere say of King Arthur, "We needs must love the highest when we see it."

As for older young people and adults, there is nothing on which to base the assumption that with maturity comes the ability to enjoy great music or art. Our admirations and our aversions—in other words, our tastes—are matters of habit. If we have learned to love jazz in childhood, we shall be still less able in adult years suddenly to become lovers of Beethoven. It is easier to change our *ideas about* things than our *feelings toward* them. So the development of appreciation of good music should begin early and be a part of the educational process all through the church school.

Contribution of Community Agencies. The public schools have done a great deal to cultivate music appreciation, through the stories of great composers and a study of musical composition, in periods devoted to appreciation lessons. The victrola and the radio have been brought into service and boys and girls have listened to beautiful music and have learned to identify certain great works and to attach the names of the composers to them. Some public schools have introduced the teaching of piano in group work and through child orchestras are cultivating the ability to play on various instruments.

In and around large cities children's symphony concerts are growing in popularity and the opportunities offered adults for musical education are increasingly available and financially possible even for those who have little to spend. There is always the radio; and "eye hath not seen, nor ear heard" what may yet be. Many of these agencies, such as the radio, bring both good and bad to us, so there is a real need for the development of standards of taste by which we may judge and choose the best for our enjoyment.

Music Appreciation in the Church. In communities where the public school or other community agencies are working to develop musical taste, the church may go ahead and build upon this splendid foundation. Churches in such communities will find children and adolescents quick to respond to periods devoted to music appreciation.

In other communities the church may have to put on a more ambitious program of music in order to raise the standards of old and young. For we must remember, that while it is more difficult for older people to change their tastes than for children, still it can be done, and any program which we may have for our boys and girls must aim to carry the fathers and mothers and the whole family along with it.

Appreciation of music must come before we can identify ourselves with its meanings. If we are really to worship through the music in a worship service, we must be able to feel what the music is saying, and we must do more than sit back and enjoy as we would at a concert, complimenting or criticizing the choir for its performance or appraising the musical technique of the organist. This is not worship. We ourselves must, through the music in the worship service, be expressing our fellowship with God or listening to his voice as he speaks to us.

Children and young people are greatly helped to feel the religious significance in the music of worship, if in some period of preparation for worship[1] they have had the musical selections enriched for them. Without this enrichment often the music is just a time to sit through until we get to something more important. In this day of pressing activity when all our emphasis is upon doing things, the art of listening needs to be cultivated.

If our worship services are upon nature themes for a few Sundays, suppose, in some period before worship, MacDowell's "To a Wild Rose" and "To a Waterlily" were interpreted to the group. Suppose the story of MacDowell's life were told and of the MacDowell colony

---

[1] See Chap. X, "Preparation for Worship."

among the New Hampshire hills, where struggling composers and artists may go and find complete rest and inspiration for their work. Let the leader tell of the sunny, grassy little inclosure on the mountainside where the American composer is buried with the flowers planted all around and the mountain winds blowing through the whispering trees. If possible, recall through some beautiful pictures in color a spot where the wild roses grow and a peaceful lily pond. In the Sundays following, when any of the above selections are used for preludes or interludes in the worship services, instead of just sitting during the musical parts of the service, the group will be actively participating because of the number of associations built up around these musical compositions.

STANDARDS BY WHICH TO TEST RELIGIOUS MUSIC

Many of us who are responsible for the religious educational program in our churches are not trained musicians. Neither are we musical critics. Our abilities in these lines vary with our educational opportunities and the use we have made of them. We can read books, attend classes, and train ourselves by listening to good music. But we need standards to guide us in our choice of music for worship. Where shall we find those standards?

Standards Given by Specialists in Field of Music. We may avail ourselves of the helps and advice of those who do understand music. This does not mean asking a musical leader, who knows nothing of our worship aims or program, to come in and conduct the musical part of the worship service as something entirely unrelated to the whole service. We are here to worship and not to study music. Such a musical specialist is our adviser and helper only. His talent should be at our disposal. We consult him that music may enrich the worship experience of the church. It would be well if such a musical consultant sat in at teachers' staff meetings when the whole problem of worship was being discussed, in order that he might see its relation to life.

Then, as we unfold before him our worship activities for succeeding Sundays, he may, out of his rich experience, suggest to us music that will suit the themes of worship. He may, occasionally, conduct periods of music appreciation, *if he has been trained* to do this, in order that *we* may learn the technique. But let us remember that many who know and understand music do not know and understand childhood and youth or the laws of pedagogy equally well. And with all their enthusiasm for their art, if they do not know how to help boys and girls *enjoy* it, an actual dislike of music may be the result.

Let us also remember that boys and girls will be more apt to appreciate that music is an integral part of worship if the leader of worship is the one who conducts the music interpretation periods. If someone else does this, it may cause a dissociation of music and worship. Besides, the one who has planned the worship service knows as no one else can what meaning he or she desires the music to contribute to the worship experience.

Standards Set by Music of Great Composers. Both for ourselves and for our children and young people it is true that by persistently staying in the presence of the best, we may gradually cultivate our taste for great art and music. And through a cultivation of a liking for the music of great composers we more or less unconsciously adopt standards by which we test the music which we hear.

Standards Set by Best Hymnals. The best way to be sure that our selection of hymn music is the best is to have in the church school the best hymnals available for each department and for the adult congregation. In *good* hymnals it is usually true that the music is composed by a number of musicians and not by one or two composers only. The good hymnals will conserve the finest hymns which have come to us out of the past, while they will also include newer hymns which express the needs and aspirations of the present day. The church should cultivate its creative artists and encourage poets and musicians to embody the religious ideals of the twentieth century in forms of beauty.

In many of the best new hymnals the contents are arranged under headings which describe the religious experience in terms of *experience* rather than in terms of theology. This practice has a tendency to relate the hymnal more closely to life. The sections in some hymnals for young people are captioned by phrases designed to seize the imagination, as: "The Quest for God," "The Great Companion," "God of the Open Spaces," "God of the City Streets," "Torch Bearers," "Knighthood's Oath and Vigil," "The House of Brotherhood," "Each in His Own Tongue."[2]

Types of Music

Music in the service of worship is for the purpose of helping the group to worship. It is not entertainment;

[2] All of the captions found in the *American Student Hymnal*, H. Augustine Smith, editor, except one, which appears in *The New Hymnal for American Youth.* Used by permission of the D. Appleton-Century Company, Inc., owners of copyright.

it is not a filler-in to cover the arrival of late-comers; it should not be a performance by a soloist or a choir, to be criticized by a listening audience. Music may serve a twofold purpose in any service. It may stimulate worship moods, generate a mystical experience, and stir the emotions. This *intake* of the spirit is one essential phase of the worship experience. But the worshiper seeks not only an intake of power; he desires also the release of energy. And through music he may *express* the feelings of worship which have been aroused. He may sing of his vision, penitence, exaltation and dedication, and as he sings, make each one of these steps more truly his own. In planning worship services this twofold function of music should be kept in mind. The music should be of such a character as to give the worshipers frequent opportunity to participate.

Instrumental Music. There is a variety of music material which may be used in worship. There is first of all the instrumental music, including preludes, interludes, and postludes; there are offertory selections and instrumental solos; and there is music which supplies the background and emotional stimulation for moments of quiet meditation.

Instrumental Solos of any kind in services for children or young people should not be so long as to outlast the span of attention, and they should be introduced into the worship service, not to provide an opportunity for some young person "to express himself," but to make a real contribution to the service. The music to be played should be decided upon with the adult leader or the worship committee, and instrumental solos introduced only on such occasions as they can best minister to the spirit of worship. It is doubtful whether a poor performer on any instrument ought to be allowed to detract from the worship experience of the group.

Anthem and Choir Selections. It is not the function of this book to consider in detail the adult worship of Sunday-morning congregations. But notice should be taken of the movement in many churches away from reliance entirely upon the services of a highly paid quartet and toward the development of chorus choirs from among the church membership. This is a movement in the direction of restoring real vitality to the experience of worship. Someone has said that music is the most human of all the arts, expressing personality in action. "As life becomes more conscious of spiritual values, it is natural to find expression in religious music. No valid church music was ever made to be listened to as a sensory pleasure. Rather, it is a collective voice uniting mankind on higher levels." So, we are not surprised that, when the early church was developing its forms of worship, liturgy and music grew up together and due provision was made for each member of the church to participate, well within his musical ability. The greater part of the music was for the minister and the people, with special provision for some trained contribution from the choir.

Some churches, in addition to the adult choir, are developing children's and young people's choirs. This often provides an opportunity for training in religious music which is invaluable to the participants. The young people in church choirs should receive not only training in music but an understanding of the purpose of worship and of the contribution which music can make to worship. They should be educated to think of their participation in the choir in terms of leadership of worship and should feel a joy and satisfaction in sharing this task with the minister or leader.

In departmental worship in the church school they can make a contribution too by leading the others and occasionally rendering a choir selection. However, the objective of our worship program is to secure the active participation in worship of every member of the department. Expression through song is one of the chief opportunities for the achievement of this goal. So we want our choirs to inspire others to share in the music and not to perform as musicians for the others to listen to.

Responses. There is one group of musical selections which we may call *responses* and *calls to worship*. There are many beautiful ones available, and a sufficient number so that we may have variety. The usual danger is that a response, once learned, is used until it has become mere words, and is sung with little thought of its meaning. Any group of any age can learn several in one year and so enrich their language of worship. Some of these take the form of calls to prayer and others are prayer responses. There are also offertory responses and benedictions for the close of worship.

The response ought to fulfill an obvious purpose in a service of worship. Sometimes a leader feels that he is making a service more worshipful by the introduction of responses at certain intervals. But unless these come at moments in the service when a response is psychologically expected or needed, they only interfere with the worship mood. One minister, in explaining to his congregation why a response was sung by the choir after the prayer, spoke of it as giving them the sensation that the aspirations of their spirits had been borne aloft on wings of song, and that their prayers had been heard.

Hymns

It is in the hymn singing that the church finds its "collective voice." For the hymn affords an opportunity for each individual to express his worshipful emotions and the feeling of each is heightened by the consciousness that every other member of the group is sharing and expressing the worship attitude with him.

Standards by Which to Test Hymns. In judging hymns the first test ought to be the *thought content.* What do the words say? For if they say the wrong things we cannot worship through them, no matter how great the music.

Hymns should convey *adequate concepts.* We have seen the importance of the concepts of God for a rich and growing worship experience.[3] Often these concepts are derived from songs or hymns.

Seumus McManus, the Irish story teller, says, "The spoken word is the remembered word." It is often true, also, that the sung word is the remembered word. Fastened in our consciousness by the power of melody, rhythm, harmony, and poetical imagery, the pictures which we sing remain with us. The symbolism of the days when God was a God of battles or a King upon a throne, is far from satisfying in our present generation, which sings:

"In wonder workings, or some bush a-flame,
   Men look for God and fancy him concealed;
   But in earth's common things he stands revealed,
While grass and flowers and stars spell out his name."[4]

We must be sure, first of all, that the hymns

---

[3] See Chap. III.
[4] Minot G. Savage, "Seek Not Afar for Beauty," from the *Hymn and Tune Book.* Copyright, The Beacon Press, Inc. Used by permission.

chosen give correct religious ideas. Poetry is always full
of pictures, and pictures, even those painted in words,
have a way of remaining with us.

We have seen how the picture which we have of Jesus
will influence our worship. There are many hymns
which suggest that there is an innate sadness about
Christianity and its spirit of sacrifice—a sadness which
certainly is not to be found in the life or spirit of its
founder. The hymns we choose for children and adolescents should paint a picture of a Jesus who was happy,
trustful, radiant in his belief in God's eternal goodness.
Boys and girls should grow up with the conviction that:

> "Never alone is the Christian
> Who lives by faith and prayer;
> For God is a friend unfailing,
> And God is everywhere."

Hymns which picture Jesus as living in such a simple,
radiant faith are the hymns which will reveal him to
children and young people as one whose personality is
so winsome that they will want to be like him.

> "We would see Jesus, on the mountain teaching,
> With all the listening people gathered round;
> While birds and flowers and sky above are preaching
> The blessedness which simple trust has found."[5]

There are other concepts too, which we may acquire
through our hymn singing, concepts of death and concepts of the whole character of the Christian life. We
want our boys and girls to have, not the pagan concept
of death, not a picture shrouded in gloom, and to be
imagined with dread. We want them to feel, as did the

---

[5] By J. Edgar Park. *The American Student Hymnal,* No. 71. The
Pilgrim Press. Used by permission.

character in Noyes' poem, that "Death was but a change of key, in life the golden melody."[6] There are very few hymns for children which contain this point of view, but we can, at least, avoid having them sing hymns which picture the sadness or horror of death.

Another test of the thought content is that hymns should contain *words and ideas within the experience of the group* using the hymn. Hymns should say, in words which each group understands, the things which those in the group truly feel. Even as the boy Jesus grew "in wisdom and stature and in favor with God and man," so do boys and girls to-day *grow* in their religious life. There are some spiritual experiences which they cannot comprehend and into which they will not enter until adolescence, and still others which will come to them only when they face the problems and broadening experiences of adult life. Some of our hymns are written for adults only; their religious meanings are entirely foreign to the child's normal attitudes and have no significance for him as he faces his everyday problems of school and play life. We do not want to make insincere Christians of them, singing with their lips phrases which they cannot possibly mean.[7] Neither do we want to sap all the meaning out of experiences for adolescents by using what are pre-eminently adolescent worship materials during the childhood years. Hymnology for later childhood is so meager in material adapted to its interests and needs that we are often obliged to use for

[6] From "The Companion of a Mile," by Alfred Noyes, *Collected Poems*, Vol. II, p. 347. Copyright, 1913, Frederick A. Stokes Company.

[7] For a treatment of hymns suitable for children see Baker, *The Worship of the Little Child*; Jones, *Training Juniors in Worship*; Blashfield, *Worship Training for Primary Children*.

children hymns which express some adolescent experience. From the standpoint of young people's worship this may seem unfortunate, as it may rob some hymns of the freshness of interest which is attached to a first approach.

But, we must not make the mistake of thinking that children or young people can never sing any hymn which they do not completely understand. While, as a usual thing, the principle of grading materials to age interests should be observed, there is such a thing as gradually growing up to the deeper meanings of some of the materials of worship.

At least one other test ought to be applied to the thought content of a hymn and that is *whether it contains a really great truth.* If we examine some so-called religious songs, we discover, by analyzing the thought, that there is very little thought in them, certainly none great enough to contribute to worship. Some songs are mere repetitions of rather unwholesome sentiments. Some writers under emotional stress descend into mere sentimentality.

The second standard by which to test hymns is the literary standard. We must appraise them as poetry. Percy Dearmer's statement, that "The object of art is not to give pleasure, as our fathers assumed, but to express the highest spiritual realities," applies to the writing of poetry as well as to the painting of a picture or the carving of a reredos screen. Our hymns seek to express in rhythmical pattern these great spiritual realities. Therefore their poetic art form should be worthy of the great religious truths which they embody.

Miss Wilkinson, herself a poet of note, tells us that poetry secures its effects through observing the laws of symmetry and variety.[8] The symmetry in poems is achieved through rhythm, rime, imagery, or symbols. In a good poem the emotion or mood of the poem must suit its rhythm. This is an excellent test to apply to our hymns when we judge them as poetry. The rhythm of Luther's great chorale, "A Mighty Fortress Is Our God," suggests by its very cadence confidence and victory. The rhythm perfectly expresses the mood of the poetry. The rhythm of "Lead, Kindly Light" makes us feel the mood of the seeker facing the unknown. In our hymnody we have a still further test to apply, for both the mood and the rhythm of the poetry must be perfectly expressed in the mood and rhythm of the music.

Another test of the literary merit of a hymn is the use of imagery and symbols. In Cardinal Newman's hymn, the symbol of the light leading on "amid the encircling gloom" is appropriate to the experience which it symbolizes. Furthermore, the symbol is sustained clear through to the end of the poem. God is not first addressed as "Light" and then later on as a King or Judge. Miss Wilkinson describes this test as "a universal truth stated in symbols that are absolutely true and appropriate."[9]

Last of all, we judge the poetry of a hymn by its diction. "The poet must use words to make truth and beauty communicable. He must use them to share life bountifully and richly. Therefore he must have a sense of the sacredness of words."

It is impossible in this brief consideration of hymns to suggest all the criteria by which to appraise the dic-

---

[8] See *New Voices*, by Marguerite Wilkinson, Part I, "The Pattern of a Poem." The Macmillan Company, New York.
[9] From *New Voices*, by Marguerite Wilkinson, p. 112. The Macmillan Company, New York. Used by permission.

tion of hymns. But, as in the use of rhythm and of symbols, the words of a hymn should accurately convey its prevailing mood. They should describe accurately the symbols or images in the poem. Those hymn writers who are true poets will avoid the use of the obvious or trite word or phrase and will try by the subtle combination of words to express universal truths in language of beauty. This does not mean that the language of hymns should be bombastic or artificial. The best poetry uses the words which are common to the life of the people of the day.

The third standard is the *musical standard*. There are some simple uses of this standard which even the untrained musician can understand and employ. *The music should be appropriate to the thought content.* This will rule out at once dance rhythms or tunes which are unsuitable media for great religious experiences. Is the music appropriate to the thought expressed in the hymn? The slow, peaceful rhythm of "Now the Day Is Over" suggests, as its words say, that the "shadows of the evening steal across the sky." The music has the sustaining quality of the prayer that the words convey and of the quiet, healing comfort that is asked from God.

If the prevailing mood of the hymn is one of joy and exaltation, the music as well as the words must express this mood. There are some moods of joy which are solemn; at other times happiness is of the more intimate everyday variety. The music should express these subtle differences in emotional tone.

We must differentiate too between music which can be enjoyed by the untrained ear of childhood and that which is appropriate for older young people. This does not mean that children must be offered cheap or jingly tunes. But, for children, the melody must be predominant. Later on the subtler combinations of harmony are enjoyed. For children, the accompaniments must be simple and subordinated to the melody. Hymns for children's voices should be pitched higher than those for older people.[10] In purchasing song books for the use of leaders in children's departments these tests should be kept in mind.

Types of Hymns. There are different types of hymns, each type making its special contribution to an all-round worship experience. Let us examine some of these types to discover how each may be the expression of religious feeling.

Of all the types which will have an appeal to youth, perhaps those which have to do with definite problems of *everyday conduct* will be the most helpful. This type of hymn affords an opportunity for the worshipers to express their dedication to the newly stimulated ideals which the worship service has aroused. Few hymns are so heartily sung by juniors and adolescents as that comparatively new one by Howard Walters, "I Would Be True." It deals with attitudes which they can understand and which they can apply in their everyday living. Hymns of this type are all too rare. There is a pressing need for more of them. Most of the hymns which do deal with conduct are phrased in abstract terms of abstract qualities rather than in terms of concrete deeds. All such hymns, if used with children, ought to be carefully prepared for by conversation, letting the children suggest the concrete deeds to which the abstract qualities

---

[10] For further suggestions, see *Worship Training for Primary Children*, by Clara Beers Blashfield. The Abingdon Press.

refer. In this way, when they sing the hymn, they will have clear-cut pictures of ways in which they can "be true" or "be brave" or "battle for the right." If they are to sing:

> "O Jesus, once a Nazareth boy,
>   And tempted like as we,
> All inward foes help us destroy
>   And spotless all to be,"

they should be helped to see what are the "inward foes" which they must destroy.

Conduct hymns may be used for all ages, but the conduct situations must be those which are real situations in the life of the group singing the hymn. Older people must prepare to meet the closing days of life with grace and calm confidence. To them, "Abide With Me" will bring comfort and strength. The kindergarten child, battling with his first fears of the dark and the unknown, will find courage to be brave in singing,

> "Need I ever know a fear?
> God, my heavenly Father's here,
>   He cares."

If our hymn singing is to be sincere, we must have hymns which are the expression of the *thinking and aspiration of our own times*. The newer religious poetry will, of course, be more apt to express these aspirations. Hymns with a social emphasis, like Frank Mason North's "Where Cross the Crowded Ways of Life," or Gilbert Chesterton's "O God of Earth and Altar," are needed to raise worship from the plane of selfish individualism to that of a brotherhood of man.

Hymns which express no narrow nationalism but which emphasize the need of Christianizing our national life will be found among the newer religious poetry. Illustrations of such hymns are Henry van Dyke's "O Lord Our God, Thy Mighty Hand,"[11] and "America Triumphant,"[12] by John Haynes Holmes. In an age that is praying for world peace, we need such hymns as John Oxenham's "In Christ There Is No East nor West," and Ozora Davis' "At Length There Dawns the Glorious Day."

The newer poetry not only expresses the aspirations of our present generation; sometimes its thoughts are clothed in language which is the language of to-day, and which visualizes the present social situation. This does not mean that we shall not use those great hymns which H. Augustine Smith calls our "Heritage Hymns."[13] Great poetry has a permanent value, and we want the enrichment of worship which comes through the best in the religious experience of the past.

In a day when nature study and the appreciation of nature are being encouraged as never before, the *nature hymn* takes an important place. God's great out-of-doors is an experience shared by young and old alike so that this type of hymn has a universal appeal. True, at different ages the world of nature means different things to us, and our choice of nature hymns throughout the departments of the church school should reflect the nature interpretations of developing lives.

This class of hymns requires little explanation to children. The world of nature every child knows and understands. He finds it easy to see God there and to believe in such tangible evidences of God's love as trees,

[11] See *The Abingdon Hymnal*, No. 231. The Abingdon Press.
[12] See *The American Student Hymnal*, No. 280. D. Appleton-Century Company, Inc.
[13] See *The American Student Hymnal*, section on "Heritage Hymns."

seashore, flowers, mountains and sunshine. Our newer hymnals are rich in exquisite hymns of this type.

One reason why nature hymns are so well liked by children is undoubtedly because they are usually so full of vivid word pictures. They describe scenes which the child can easily imagine, familiar things and places which he has seen. And, indeed, those of us who are older enjoy them for the same reasons.

Often we express our *prayers* in hymn form. Here we must guard against insincerity in worship by seeing that in children's groups the hymns voice desires native to a child, and not adult hopes and aspirations. On the other hand, adolescents and adults have outgrown some of the more childish prayer hymns.

Prayer is apt to become meaningless, if it is always offered in the same way, and the prayer which is sung will sometimes mean as much as the one which is said. Such hymns may well follow the story in the service of worship and be the outward expression of the inward feeling. Sometimes such a hymn may be used as a response after the prayer has been offered; or it may be sung softly before the prayer to focus the attention of the group and prepare them for the attitude of prayer. Examples of such are "Hear Us, Our Father," "For the Beauty of the Earth," "We Thank Thee, O Our Father," "God of the Earth, the Sky, the Sea," and "Father, Lead Me Day by Day."

Often just one verse of a hymn is a prayer, and in such cases the group should be led to note the difference between the way in which such a verse should be sung and all the others. In the hymn "We Plow the Fields," only the third verse is a prayer. The first two tell of God as the Creator of all things. Then the worshiper, after thinking of all the wonderful blessings which God showers upon the world, bursts forth into a song of gratitude:

> "We thank thee, then, O Father,
> For all things bright and good."

Not all prayer hymns are to be sung softly and quietly. Some of them are as vigorous as the blessings for which they ask or the aspirations which they express. Note, for instance, the vigor, yet solemnity, of this great hymn:

> "God of our Fathers, whose almighty hand
> Leads forth in beauty all the starry band
> Of shining worlds in splendor through the skies,
> Our grateful songs before thy throne arise."

Other prayer hymns that are majestic and vigorous are "O God, Beneath Thy Guiding Hand," and "Father, Hear the Prayer We Offer."

In selecting hymns with a *missionary* emphasis, we are face to face with the necessity of scrutinizing them in the light of some of the newer approaches to the missionary enterprise. We have long ago outgrown the attitude of superiority over other races. We recognize that our hymns should emphasize the worth of other races and the essential similarities of all races instead of the differences. But we have further still to go in a day when the very motives for the spread of Christianity are being examined. Let us watch for a new hymnology to express developing trends in missions.

Perhaps we shall be helped toward a more perfect feeling of union with other races if we occasionally use the worship materials of other races. If the youth of the world can worship together through common worship materials, we may expect to have a real House of Brotherhood.

Since music is a universal language, it can obliterate differences and bind worshipers of many races and religious faiths together in a fellowship of understanding. As we worship through the music of other races we can feel our kinship with all of God's children. Protestant churches have a wonderful heritage in the great religious music which has come down through the Roman Catholic Church. Many hymnals contain hymns which have come to us through this tradition.[14]

Adeste Fidelis—Latin hymn, seventeenth century.
All Creatures of Our God and King—Saint Francis of Assisi, 1225.
All Glory, Laud, and Honor—Theodulph of Orleans, c. 820.
A Mighty Fortress Is Our God—Martin Luther, 1529.
Fairest Lord Jesus—German, seventeenth century.
Father, We Praise Thee—Gregory the Great, 540-604.
Jerusalem the Golden—Bernard of Cluny, 1145.
Jesus, the Very Thought of Thee—Latin, eleventh century.
Lead, Kindly Light—Cardinal Newman, 1833.
Now With Creation's Morning Song—Aurelius Clemens Prudentius, fifth century.
O Splendor of God's Glory Bright—Ambrose of Milan, 340-397.
Shepherd of Tender Youth—Clement of Alexandria, 220 A. D.
The Day of Resurrection—John of Damascus, eighth century.
The Strife Is O'er—Anon. Latin to music by Palestrina.
Welcome, Happy Morning—Gregory the Great, 540-604.

With the adolescent years come the choice of a life-work and the frank facing of the necessity for all sorts of choices. The expanding self sees the vision and hears the call to "Follow the Gleam." At this period, above all

[14] These hymns may be found in one of the following hymnals, as well as in many others: *The Abingdon Hymnal*, The Abingdon Press. *Church School Hymnal for Youth*, Presbyterian Board of Christian Education. *New Hymnal for American Youth*, D. Appleton-Century Company.

others, there is need for hymns which express the thought of the dedication of life. Hymns of this kind should not be sung when there is no sense of dedication to a high destiny. But the properly guided worship experience of adolescence ought to culminate in a deeper sense of one-ness with God and his purposes.

> "Just as I am, thine own to be,
> Friend of the young, who lovest me,
> To consecrate myself to thee,
> O Jesus Christ, I come."

I Am Your Hymnal[15]

BY P. R. HAYWARD

I am your Hymnal.

I spend my days in the rack in front of you or on the seat beside you and I am always at your command.

When you reach for me I am always there, ready to open at your will.

By the mystery of the printer's art I have shared the wisdom and the ideals of the ages and hold them in store ready to let them leap, at your will, from my pages to nestle in your responsive heart.

The beautiful vision of the poets, the heart-throbs of the mystics, the dreams of the prophets, and the constructive purpose of the social pioneer—all these are mine—to be made yours.

Men of your own faith, and those of other great faiths, broaden your life as they speak to you through me.

By the strange art of printed signs and symbols great music has been captured as it overflowed the souls of the musicians of all time and is released from me to tremble in the air about you and enter your life.

I am your Hymnal.

The Use of Music in Worship

In planning for the use of music in worship, the law of variety is as important as it is in the planning of

---

[15] Used by permission of the author.

other features. When there is little musical talent available, the musical part of the worship service will necessarily be very simple, but even with few musical resources, the element of variety can be introduced, though it may be only in the singing of hymns.

The Musical Prelude. Ordinarily, the opening prelude precedes the call to worship and is itself the first step in preparing the group for worship. In some church situations it requires education to establish the habit of silent meditation the moment the prelude begins, but even when worshipers have learned to sit quietly through the opening music, their thoughts may be far away from the theme of worship. On some occasion the piano or organ might play for a few moments and then cease or play very softly while the leader rises and repeats Tennyson's "Flower in the Crannied Wall." Then, he might say, "Perhaps MacDowell, our American composer, felt the same mystery at the heart of the universe as he watched the wild roses blooming over some New England wall. Let us attempt to think God's thoughts after him as we listen to MacDowell's music, 'To a Wild Rose.'"

The Offertory. In much the same way, groups may be helped to worship during the offertory by some arresting comment from the leader which builds up in the mind of the worshipers some association between the act of giving and the music which is being played. In order to sustain attention in younger groups which have not yet attained adult control of their thoughts and actions, the offertory music may be interpreted and appreciated in a previous period of preparation, or imagination may be stimulated just before the offertory. The leader might say something like this:

"Our morning's offering is going to far places of the world to help our missionary pioneers bring comfort and health and happiness to countless people. As we listen to the music, let us send our thought out across the seas to lonely places where brave men and women think of the homes they have left behind them. Let us remember the new homes they are establishing with joy in the countries of their adoption. Let us send out thoughts of encouragement to the pioneers of the world."

> "Think you that aerial wires
>   Whisper more than spirits may?
> Think you that our strong desires
>   Touch no distance when we pray?
> Never doubt that they'll receive it;
> Send it once and you'll believe it."[16]

Associating Music With Other Worship Materials. The synchronizing of music with other worship materials is one way of enriching the worship experience. It is possible to associate music with Scripture in such a way that both gain a richer meaning. For instance, the vision of the young prophet Isaiah might be read, with a pause after each of the steps in his worship experience, while the mood is expressed in music.

Scripture: Isaiah 6. 1-4, The Vision of God.
  Music: "Sanctus," by Gounod, sung by choir.
Scripture: Isaiah 6. 5, Humility.
  Music: "Father, O Hear Us," by Handel,[17] played or sung; or "O Lord of Love Compassionate."[18]

---

[16] From "Wireless," by Alfred Noyes, in *Collected Poems,* Vol. III. Copyright, 1919, Frederick A. Stokes Company.
[17] For a simplified arrangement see *Church School Hymnal for Youth,* p. 317. Presbyterian Board of Christian Education.
[18] Miserere Nobis, *The American Student Hymnal,* p. 398.

Scripture: Isaiah 6. 6-7, Forgiveness and Vitality.
  Music: Chant, Psalm 103.[19]
Scripture: Isaiah 6. 8a, Illumination.
  Music: "Send Out Thy Light."
Scripture: Isaiah 6. 8b, The Response of Dedication.
  Music: Unison singing of the hymn, "The Voice of
    God Is Calling," with emphasis upon the verse:
      "We heed, O Lord, thy summons,
        And answer, 'Here are we!'
      Send us upon thy errand,
        Let us thy servants be."[20]

There are other Scripture selections which may be
linked with music, as the Beatitudes or the separate
petitions of the Lord's Prayer. Where choirs are not
available, services may be worked out by correlating
hymns with Scripture. For instance, the hymn, "We
Would See Jesus," lends itself to interpretation by both
Scripture and pictures.

Verse 1. "We would see Jesus, lo his star is shining."
  Scripture: Luke 2. 1-20.
  Pictures: Correggio, "Holy Night"; W. L. Taylor,
    "O Little Town of Bethlehem"; LeRolle, "The
    Adoration of the Shepherds."

Verse 2. "We would see Jesus . . . ,
            Light of the village life from day to day."
  Scripture: Luke 2. 39-52.
  Pictures: Millais, "Jesus in the Home of His Par-
    ents"; Murillo, "Joseph and the Child Jesus."

[19] For arrangement of this chant, see *The American Student
Hymnal*, No. 394.
[20] By John Haynes Holmes, in *Church School Hymnal for Youth*,
p. 284.

Verse 3. "We would see Jesus on the mountain teaching."
> Scripture: Selections from the Sermon on the Mount.
> Pictures: Copping, "The Sermon on the Mount"; Burnand, "The Sermon on the Mount."

Verse 4. "We would see Jesus in the early morning."
> Scripture: Mark 1. 16-20; Matthew 9. 9.
> Pictures: Zimmerman, "Jesus and the Fishermen"; Armitage, "Christ Calling James and John"; William Hole, "Follow Me."

There are many ways in which music can be synchronized with *pictures*. Further suggestions will be found in other chapters of this book.[21]

MUSICAL LEADERSHIP IN WORSHIP

Many churches do not avail themselves of all the musical resources which are at their disposal in developing an appreciation of religious music among young and old in the church. Some church organists are quite capable of conducting simple programs in which the messages of musical selections are interpreted and then played, while even the youngest listens to see "what the music is saying." In church-school departments the pianist often can do this sort of thing in appreciation periods.

The Service of the Pianist. Not too much can be said about the very important service which the pianist can render in the worship program. The leader of worship should share his plans for worship with the pianist.

[21] See Chap. VI and Chap. X. Also Blashfield, *Worship Training for Primary Children*, Chap. V.

MUSIC IN WORSHIP

Whenever the latter is an experienced musician he can suggest musical selections which are appropriate for different worship themes. In case such an experienced person is not available, many of the good hymnals contain brief sections of musical numbers suitable for worship.

But even the least experienced pianist can be made to feel that his contribution is an important one, and he can be trained to be alert, to be ready to play musical interludes of a few bars during the transitions from one part of a service to another and to acquire a reverent spirit which seeks to use the gift of music to stimulate genuine feelings of worship.

Whenever possible the pianist should be able to play accurately and with assurance. He should have a fine sense of rhythm and time and understand the special technique of playing hymns. He should be able, through his playing, to lead the group and keep it to the rhythm of the hymns. He should study the hymns so as to adapt the tempo and the volume to the thought content of each verse.

The leader of worship should have a copy of the entire service of worship ready for the pianist, preferably a week or several days in advance. There should be a clearly understood agreement as to the times during the service when music is desired, as to how much of the hymn is to be played before the singing and as to whether the hymns are to conclude with an "Amen." A good general rule to be observed is to add the "Amen" to all hymns which address God or are of a distinctly prayer type. Co-operation of this kind between the leader and the pianist will tend to make the service of worship run smoothly.

ADDITIONAL READING SOURCES

Benson, L. F., *The Hymnody of the Christian Church*. Harper & Brothers.

Coleman, Satis M., *Creative Music in the Home*. Chautauqua Trade Products, Valparaiso, Ind.

Colson, Elizabeth, *Hymn Stories*. The Pilgrim Press.

Dickinson, Edward, *The Spirit of Music*. Charles Scribner's Sons.

Harper, Earl E., *Church Music and Worship*. The Abingdon Press.

Harrington, Karl Pomeroy, *Education in Church Music*. D. Appleton-Century Co.

Lightwood, James T., *Hymn Tunes and Their Story*. The Epworth Press, London.

McAll, Reginald L., *Practical Church School Music*. The Abingdon Press.

Surette, Thomas W., *Music and Life*. Houghton Mifflin Company.

Children's Hymnals:

Adams, Mrs. Crosby, *Worship Songs for the Sunday School and Home*. Clayton F. Summy, Chicago.

Baker, Clara Belle, and Kohlsaat, Caroline, *Songs for the Little Child*. The Abingdon Press.

Blashfield, Cora Beers, *Song Friends for Younger Children*. The Vaile Company.

Danielson, Frances W., *Song and Play for Children*. Pilgrim Press.

Danielson, Frances W., and Conant, Grace W., *Songs for Little People*. Pilgrim Press.

Presbyterian Board of Christian Education, *Primary Music and Worship*.

Presbyterian Board of Christian Education, *Junior Church School Hymnal*.

Shields, Elizabeth McE., *Worship and Conduct Songs*. Presbyterian Committee of Publication, Richmond, Va.

Thomas, Edith Lovell, *A First Book in Hymns and Worship*. The Abingdon Press.

Hymnals for Older Groups:

Dickie, Mary S., *Singing Pathways*. Powell & White.

Harper, Earl E., *The Abingdon Hymnal*. The Abingdon Press.

MUSIC IN WORSHIP

Littlefield, M. S., and Slattery, Margaret, *The Hymnal for Young People.* A. S. Barnes.

Presbyterian Board of Christian Education, *Church School Hymnal for Youth.*

Smith, H. Augustine, *American Student Hymnal.* D. Appleton-Century Company.

Smith, H. Augustine, *New Hymnal for American Youth.* D. Appleton-Century Company.

CHAPTER IX

PRAYER IN WORSHIP

> The builder who first bridged Niagara's gorge,
> Before he swung his cable, shore to shore,
> Sent out across the gulf his venturing kite
> Bearing a slender cord for unseen hands
> To grasp upon the further cliff and draw
> A greater cord and then a greater yet;
> Till at last across the chasm swung
> The cable—then the mighty bridge in air!
>
> So we may send our little timid thought
> Across the void, out to God's reaching hands—
> Send out our love and faith to thread the deep—
> Thought after thought until the little cord
> Has greatened to a chain no chance can break,
> And we are anchored to the Infinite!
>
> —EDWIN MARKHAM.
>
> (From "Anchored to the Infinite," in *The Shoes of Happiness*, p. 104. Doubleday, Doran and Company.)

WHEN we speak of "prayer in worship," we do not mean to imply that prayer is only one incident in the total experience of worship. What is meant is that prayer is, in *some* form, in all of worship, for prayer *is* worship. Prayer is the assuming of a direct and personal relationship to God. It is fellowship with him; sharing his thoughts and attitudes and purposes. It is the fruition of worship.

This fellowship may take on different forms. It may be a permeating consciousness of the presence of God which is with us all through a service of worship, even when we are not engaged in that part of the ritual which is designated as Prayer. This same "practice of the

presence of God" may be with us at other times than in
a service of worship. We may be conscious of our fellowship with God while in the midst of the activities of
life. Such a fellowship will often be characterized by
swift movements of the spirit toward God, by brief
direct expressions of our desires or appreciation. This
constant, all-pervading consciousness of God's presence,
which is itself a sort of communion, is one form of
prayer.[1]

But there is also that other type of prayer-fellowship
in which the individual is engaging in a conscious activity at a stated time—an activity which is a direct
approach to God. These two types of prayer, that of a
constant attitude and that of a conscious activity occur-
ring at a stated time, are indissolubly bound together.
But in this chapter we are chiefly concerned with the
latter type.

Writers on the subject of prayer describe differently
the various steps in prayer, but all speak of the far-
reaching possibilities involved in effective prayer. Undoubtedly, if we stopped to think of it, we should realize
how rich and full the lives of men and women and young
people might be if they understood and were in the
habit of using the power of prayer. We should realize
too what spiritual energies might be released for the
building of the City of God, if prayer were a more vital
force in the lives of Christians.

The Significance of Prayer

Since worship reaches its highest culmination in this
direct communion with God, which we call prayer, the

---

[1] See *The Life of Prayer in a World of Science*, p. 51, by William
Adams Brown.

significance of prayer in worship is very far-reaching. To plan for the expression of the worshipers' personalities through prayer will tax all of the resources of the leader's own personality. To venture to guide others into a satisfying and enriching prayer experience requires a courage dauntless enough to force a leader to make rigorous demands upon himself by way of preparation.

Difficulties in a Scientific Age. There are certain obstacles which often interfere with a satisfying prayer life, and any leader of worship ought to do his utmost to remove any such obstacles in his own experience. There is a wealth of literature on the subject of prayer written by those who have had deep and satisfying experiences of prayer. Familiarity with this literature ought to be part of any leader's preparation for worship.

One of the obstacles to belief in the efficacy of prayer is the questioning spirit which is one of the by-products of our scientific age. The attitude of questioning may be of help if it leads us on to explore new meanings of prayer and if it awakens in us that "expectancy" of which William Adams Brown speaks, urging us to "accept each experience that comes to us not as ultimate, but as a door opening into a new and larger world."[2]

But the scientific method does raise questions which engender doubt and thus inhibit the experience of worship. And many a layman in the field of science questions without having the reassurance which familiarity with the background and findings of modern science gives. For, says Doctor Brown, "Scientists are recovering the attitude of anticipation which religion has lost." "[The scientist] finds it easy to have faith because

[2] *The Life of Prayer in a World of Science*, p. 128.

so many things have come to pass which once seemed impossible."

Necessity of Preparation for Leadership in Prayer. The whole question of the history of prayer, of the rational basis for a belief in its power, and of the psychology of prayer is too vast to receive adequate treatment in a general course on worship. But every leader of worship should have a course on the subject of prayer, and should, by reading and study, clarify his thinking about prayer—as a preparation for his task of leading others in worship.

Necessity for Reality in Prayer. The leader of worship must not only study *about* prayer. He must have a first-hand experience of prayer, if he would guide others through that experience. Prayer must be a reality to the leader if it is to be real to the worshiping group. The very manner and tone of voice in which some people pray convey to those who are listening a sense of the reality or the unreality of the experience.

THE CONTENT OF PRAYER

After reading and thinking about the meaning of prayer and what it can do to strengthen the chain by which "we are anchored to the Infinite,"[3] we are ready to ask ourselves what ought to be the content of our prayers. What shall we put into our prayers to make them the kind that will endow us with power to live the Christian life?

Appreciation. Appreciation is one of the finest flowers of the spiritual life. If, as the little girl said, "We have worship to be friends with God," it is natural that

---

[3] Edwin Markham, *Shoes of Happiness*, p. 104. Doubleday, Doran and Company.

we should express appreciation of all that God means to us.

We cannot think of God as being so self-centered as to be gratified by the praise of his children. We do not want to ascribe to him any attitudes which we would deem unworthy in ourselves. But the finest living relationships flourish only in an atmosphere of appreciation of personality by personality. And we shall find it natural to express to God our appreciation of his world and our part in it, for the beauty, love, and friendships of life, for the opportunities of rich and fruitful living.

There will be one guiding principle in the development of our own personal prayer life as well as in the development of the prayer life of our groups. That is the principle of *improvement*. Like the whole worship experience of which it is a part, prayer will need to be a growing experience. Our aim will be to lift our prayers to higher and higher levels of thought and feeling.

No surer test of the status of our religious living will be found than in the nature of those things for which we express appreciation and gratitude in our prayers. By this, we mean, the *real* prayers of the inner mind. While children are usually first grateful for material things which they can see, hear, touch, smell, or taste, it is possible for even very little children to feel appreciation for the inner meanings of things and for the spiritual laws which make life noble and truly happy.

Joyce Kilmer, the poet, can sing,

> "Thank God for the stress and pain of life,
> And oh, thank God for God!"[4]

---

[4] From the poem, "Thanksgiving," in *Poems, Essays, and Letters*, Vol. I, p. 152, by Joyce Kilmer. Copyright, 1914, 1918, by Doubleday, Doran and Company, Inc. Used by permission.

And a little boy of five can pray, "Thank you for putting Jesus into the world to help us know what is right to do, and thank you for You, because you can guard us better than anybody else."[5]

Confession. It is interesting that one of the oldest practices of the Christian Church is to-day being recognized as a primary need for fruitful living. There is a cleansing power in the confession of weakness or wrongdoing which releases the one who confesses from hindrances which block his path to happy co-operation with God. Psychologists, psychotherapists, and ministers unite in their testimony to the value of confession.[6] Often it is helpful to share the burden of our confession with another human soul, one who can reassure us and help us to realize God's forgiveness. But in our private prayers we can do much to free ourselves from not only sin, but "worry, fear, sorrow, and disappointment."[7]

In corporate worship there is a recognition of this fundamental human need in the prayer of confession which in some communions comes early in the service of worship and which is followed by the prayer of absolution or a declaration of forgiveness. Thousands of troubled souls have found comfort and a cleansing vitality in the beautiful General Confession which has come down to us through the Anglican tradition and which to-day is often used by churches of other denominations.

Petition. To many worshipers, prayer has been thought of mainly as petition. With a concept of God

---

[5] From *Children's Prayers: Recorded by Their Mother*, p. 43. The Pilgrim Press.
[6] See Weatherhead, *Psychology in the Service of the Soul*. The Macmillan Company.
Oliver, *Psychiatry and Mental Health*. Charles Scribner's Sons.
Lichliter, *The Healing of Souls*. The Abingdon Press.
Gilkey, *Managing One's Self*. The Macmillan Company.
[7] Weatherhead, p. 83.

as an autocratic dispenser of good and evil, prayer will naturally assume the aspect of asking for things. But with more adequate concepts of God, prayer becomes the sharing experience of a great friendship.

Some writers to-day feel that petition has no place in prayer. But if we turn again to the analogy of a great friendship, we recognize that one feels free to ask for help or guidance from a real friend. The very fact that we *ask* means that we have put ourselves into an attitude of receptivity and expectancy, so that God can speak to us in answer to our prayer.

"Ask and ye shall receive" is a psychological fact as well as a spiritual truth. But as in the case of our appreciations, so here the aim is to raise our desires to higher and higher levels and to recognize, with Fosdick, that no matter what the lips may utter, prayer is "dominant desire."

Even little children can be trained from the beginning to ask not for material "things," but for guidance for themselves, for help to live in right relations to others, and even for great causes.

What we *desire* will largely depend upon what we appreciate. The individual who is brought up to enjoy and appreciate a rich experience will have a surer basis for communion with God.

Aspiration. One effect of a great friendship is to stimulate in us a desire to be like our friend or to live up to what he expects of us. Aspiration is characteristic of all real fellowship with God. The whole worship experience arouses in us new impulses and desires.

It is the fleeting aspect of many of these impulses which often troubles us in our endeavor to live the good life. In prayer we hold them before our own attention

as well as express them to God. We reaffirm our resolve
to let these aspirations control our daily living. Leslie
D. Weatherhead says that one of the values of prayer is
its power to fire the will with feeling. When we express
our aspirations in prayer, we feel that we are indeed
sharing a life of the spirit with God. If we pour out
our personal desires to live life more courageously, more
radiantly, more unselfishly, we *feel* that we are by so
doing helping to express God's purpose for us, and we
also feel that in the very expression of our desire we are
laying hold of God's own power.

The richest prayer life is that in which the worshiper
finds himself more and more interpreting his aspirations
in terms of identifying himself with God's purposes for
bringing in the kingdom of God. "Not my will but
thine" represents the highest expression of man's aspiration for spiritual achievement.

Dedication. If prayer means anything at all, it means
then dedication to fulfill in actual living the newly
roused aspirations to be like God, our Father. To be a
child of God is not only a gift but an achievement. In
this sense prayer is creative. It makes us over into persons with a new will to do. It generates the creative
forces which will through our personalities touch other
lives and make human society better.

Wonder. The questioning spirit of a scientific age
may push us on to seek explanations of what we do not
understand, but the true scientist, no matter to what far
limits he pushes his experiments, stands forever on the
brink of wonder. God may be thought of as a real
Presence, a Power pervading all of life, but he is forever
a mystery as well. Miss Stevens, writing of the value of
universe-study for children, says: "The wonder of the

world should take hold of children, not as miracle or magic, but as rational successions of events uncovered increasingly by science, and leading thought on to the great How and Why which science never tries to answer. In the words of Mr. Thomson, the sense of wonder is one of the saving graces of life; and if it dies, he says, one of the lights of life goes out."[8]

It is natural, then, and desirable that our prayers shall express our feeling of wonder at the great mysteries of life.

CHARACTERISTICS OF PRAYER

Although prayer is the very heart of worship and the culmination of the God-communion experience, a study of the attitudes and conduct of children and of adolescents during prayer will reveal the fact that often they are worshiping less during the prayers in a worship service than during any other part of the service. Let us see if we can discover the reasons for this, and let our discoveries reveal what must be the characteristics of prayer if it is to be vital.

Brevity. *Prayers should be brief.* The span of child attention is not long. In fact, attention, at any age, cannot be held for long on one unvarying object. Stories and hymns are characterized by movement, rhythm, emphasis; and by this variety of appeal they hold the attention.

Prayers should continue only so long as attention is given to them. Otherwise insincerity will result. Two or three sentences will suffice to hold the attention of a primary child. And not much longer should be prayers for juniors, if they are offered for the group by an adult

---

[8] From *Child and Universe*, p. 10. The John Day Company, Inc. Used by permission.

leader. Prayers said in unison may be somewhat longer, since the participants are actively engaged in the prayer-process.

It is doubtful how well adolescents and adults can hold their attention upon prayers of any length. Attempts have been made to estimate the span of adult attention during worship and, according to one of these tests, five minutes was the longest period of adult attention, while many found their thoughts wandering after a shorter time.

To say what needs to be said in a few sentences or a short paragraph is far more difficult than to ramble on using many words. This is one reason why prayers should be carefully thought out beforehand and not attempted without preparation.

Experience of the Group. *Prayer should relate to the experience of the group.* If the objectives of our worship services are to help individuals live as children of God and in fellowship with him in their own life situations, then it follows that the prayers in the worship services will refer to specific situations which are real to the worshipers. For we have already seen how in following the principle of unity[9] in building the worship service, prayer to be effective will express in terms of aspiration and dedication the objective of the service. This is one reason why prayer is more meaningful when it arises naturally as a group is pursuing some interest or carrying out an activity.

Though prayers offered in a planned worship service lack the spontaneity of those which arise in some life-activity, they may relate closely to the experiences which are of most concern to the group at the time. Let us

---

[9] See Chap. IV, "Planning the Service of Worship."

remember that these experiences need not be narrowly personal, but may be of a socially expansive nature.

Byington suggests that if the leader is to secure the attention of the group, the prayer should commence where the worshipers are in their thinking. If some matter of public concern is the subject of thought and conversation, some reference to it in the opening sentences of the prayer will enable the leader to start with the prevailing thought of the group. This is a bit of sound psychology which any leader of prayer may do well to use. It is only one more suggestion as to the need of knowing the present needs and problems of any group in order to make the service of worship minister to those interests.

Specific Prayer. *Prayer should be specific.* One reason for the unreality of much prayer is its vagueness and its generalness. Prayers expressing desire for specific attitudes or dedication to specific tasks will do much to make prayer vital and interesting. And without *interest* prayer is futile.

Perhaps we need to observe one caution at this point. Prayers can be so specific as to shut out some worshipers in the group, because their special needs or interests are not included. This should be kept in mind especially when planning worship for older groups. But the prayer which relates specifically to the objectives of the worship service will be more heartfelt and vital than a prayer which is too general or which covers too wide a range of interests.

Concrete Imagery in Prayer. Undoubtedly one reason why children often do not worship during prayer is that while our stories and many of our hymns are full of concrete pictures, the moment we start to pray we use abstract words. Children, we have seen, do not comprehend abstract statements of truth. They need to see goodness at work in concrete situations or lived out by people. Prayers for children, then, should be full of "pictures," so that the child's mind is at every moment of the prayer visualizing his expressions of appreciation, aspiration, petition, or dedication.

We have only to listen to the spontaneous prayers of a five-year-old to see how concretely his mind works and how God's goodness is not something vague to him, but is expressed in very specific things.

"Thank you for everything that you have made, for you are so good to everybody and like to do things for them. Thank you for grass and trees and flowers, and for bread and milk, and for all our good food, and for flowers that grow in people's gardens, and for trees to climb. Thank you for mothers and daddies that make things for us, like bows and arrows to shoot with, and thank you for Indians to be friendly with, and for Eskimos and everybody in the world—and thank you for our happy days.[10]

But adolescents too enjoy concreteness of imagery to make their prayers vivid and real. In the following prayer for a group of adolescents in camp, note the vivid word pictures, as well as the simplicity, beauty and dignity of the language.

"God of forest and field, for a little time we, thy children, are dwellers in tents, as Abraham was. Let these nights in the open bless not only our bodies but our minds and hearts as well. When we sleep, let us rest. Should we chance to wake in the night, let us feel the

---

[10] From *Children's Prayers*, by Darr, pp. 42,43. Copyright, The Pilgrim Press. Used by permission.

companionship of the cool, clean wind, the beauty of the sentinel stars, the significance of all the faint sounds, the pungent airs that stir in the summer night. Sleeping or waking, may we realize thy guardian Presence among our tents. And when the day breaks may we not fail to know that Presence still.

"Lord of the wide spaces and of the solemn woods, make us worthy to camp out in thine open with thee!"[11]

The Language of Prayer. Sometimes boys and girls (and young people too) fail to listen to a prayer or to participate in a unison prayer because the language is not that which seems natural to them. This does not mean that we must drop into the vernacular in our praying or use language which is undignified. Children respond to beauty, and there are some beautiful form prayers which they will enjoy using. It is interesting too to note how in composing original prayers boys and girls will make conscious attempts to clothe their prayers in beautiful language.

But prayers offered by leaders ought to sound spontaneous and natural, conveying the feeling that the one praying is actually talking to God and not for the benefit of an audience. This type of prayer will sound *most* natural, if it is really thought out beforehand very carefully. To wait for the inspiration of the moment will usually mean a prayer which does not realize the possibilities of the worship service or reach the group.

Variety in Prayer. To keep the prayer experience fresh and vital, there should be some variety in the content and form of prayers, as well as in the methods of introducing them into the worship service.

---

[11] From *The Atlantic Readers,* Book III, p. 81. Little, Brown & Company.

A very beautiful prayer may fall upon unlistening ears if its form or the method of introducing it into the service is similar to that used on countless other occasions. The leader of worship must ask himself, "How can I introduce the experience of prayer into this service of worship in such a way as to arrest the attention of the worshipers so that they may participate wholeheartedly and make the prayer their own?" Let us see what are some of the methods of introducing prayer into worship, so that it may be a vital part of the total worship experience.

METHODS OF USING PRAYER IN WORSHIP

In deciding which methods of prayer to use in a given service the leader will have to keep in mind, first of all, the age group which is participating in the service. Periods of silent meditation, for instance, are not so easily handled for children as for adults and older young people. There have been some interesting experiments in quiet periods for children but these need to be conducted by those who understand the psychology of childhood or by groups like the Quakers, whose habitual form of worship is after this pattern.[12]

There are certain types of prayer which will not be used when old and young are worshiping together. Prayers for such groups may vary in form, length, and style of language from those used in more closely graded assemblies.

There may be a difference in the type of prayer which is helpful in large groups of worshipers from that which is effective for the worship of smaller, more intimate

[12] *As Children Worship*, by Jeannette E. Perkins. The Pilgrim Press.

groups. So, the leader will need to discover, by study and by practice, the method of prayer which will give most vitality to each worship experience.

Prayer by the Leader for the Group. This type of prayer may be offered by the adult for the group, by a young person in meetings of adolescents, and, under just the right conditions, by a child in his own department. The older leader who attempts this ought to be fully conscious of the difficulties involved in trying to make this type of prayer real. It is not easy to be sure that one is voicing the desires of a group of people. It is not easy to express the prayer in language which will appeal to them. To offer prayer for a group requires earnest preparation, not only of the prayer itself, but of the mood of the leader. Any indications that individuals in a group are not following the prayer with a sense of concern ought to suggest to those who are planning the worship services that the problem of prayer be studied with a view to discovering *why* there is lack of attention or participation.

If young people are to lead in prayer, their leadership will be more effective if it is preceded by a study and discussion of the meaning, the content, and the forms of prayer.

Since the problem of child leadership in prayer is one which pertains to child groups alone, superintendents of children's departments ought to study the departmental worship units and read what successful workers with children have to say about this. In general, the testimony is that this method achieves results which are helpful to childhood when it is the outcome of an educational procedure which enlists children in the planning and initiation of their learning experiences, so that planning for the prayer in their worship services occasionally is as natural and unself-conscious an act as is all their other educational experience.[13]

Unison Prayers. Unison prayers may be read from prayer books, mimeographed sheets, or hymnals, or they may be recited from memory. Of course very little children cannot handle papers or books with ease and without having their attention drawn from the meaning of the worship service. Older children are somewhat more able to do this, but will manage better if they are trained in the use of such materials. Some church schools have used "Books of Worship"—notebooks into which mimeographed copies of prayers, hymns, and responses are pasted, so that the pupils have a sort of prayer book to supplement the hymnal.

There are distinct values in the memorizing of some beautiful prayers. But, as boys and girls grow older, in order to keep prayer fresh and vital, it is necessary to use more prayers than the group can possibly memorize. Some of the unison prayers may be used for a season and then resumed after an interval and in this way be retained in memory.

Prayers Composed by Group Suggestion. This method of developing prayer offers a very real opportunity to make prayer vital, especially to children or to young people in small groups. By this method the leader asks the group for suggestions of what shall go into the prayer. Sometimes the leader takes these suggestions and weaves them together into a prayer. Occasionally individuals in the group may take the suggestions and embody them in written prayers. Some of these

---

[13] See *And Others Call it God,* by Jeannette E. Perkins. Harper and Brothers.

finished prayers may be brought back to the group for reading and appreciation and later for use in worship.

The group composition of prayers may take place in the worship service itself, especially if it is a service of the less formal type. Or the method may be used in a period of preparation for worship. The latter will be the case when the pupils are to experiment with the suggestions and put them into written prayers.

Sometimes the creation of group prayers may occur in a class period, when, in the exchange of ideas in a small group, it is easier to solve the difficulties in the prayer life and to be sure that the prayer is the work of the whole group.

Individual Prayers by Pupils. There are some church departments in which the children begin at a very early age to offer spontaneous prayers. There is certainly a place in the worship experience for this spontaneous expression of our attitudes toward God. This method has the advantage of helping the individual to acquire habits of prayer. But it should be spontaneous and never forced. Such prayers should not provide an opportunity for individual pupils to "show off" before others.

Prayers by individual pupils occur most naturally in small groups, where a feeling of warm fellowship has been established and where there is an utter lack of self-consciousness.

Many an adult devotional meeting has been robbed of its devotional quality by the spontaneous prayers of those who pray too long, or too monotonously, or who, for some other reason, fail to carry the group along with them. Often there has been no preparation on the part of the one praying. Young people's services have suf-

fered too from the "sentence prayers" which would have
been far more effective had those participating been told
beforehand something about the nature of the worship
service and about the theme and asked to embody some
aspect of the theme in their prayers.

Spontaneous prayer to reach its fullest possibilities of
helpfulness ought probably to be brief, and to be the
inevitable expression of group desire which is the out-
growth of co-operative worship. When we have thought
through a problem together, trying to discover a common purpose in the purpose of God, then we may each
express in prayer our purpose as a member of the group
or we may voice the common aspiration of all. This
type of spontaneous prayer by the individual is thus not
unprepared prayer. It has been prepared by the group-
thinking which has preceded it. There is a real opportunity for the minister to make the mid-week prayer
meeting over into this type of creative, co-operative
worship.

In children's groups this type of praying is always
prepared for by informal conversation or the telling of a
story which stimulates the thinking and feeling of the
boys and girls and reveals the common purpose of the
group.

Silent Prayer. In the older departments in the
church, there is an opportunity for a greater use of
silence in worship. After all, the real objective of worship is to stimulate each individual to acquire the
practice of worship. This can be accomplished in part
by making a place in some of the worship services for
periods of quiet meditation. Since the very heart of the
worship experience is the realization of God and communion with him, there ought to be opportunities

occasionally when the worshiper can be quiet and know that God is there.

We may also utilize brief moments of silence in the midst of other activities. A group of young people around an open fire after an informal discussion may listen to a brief devotional talk, a poem, a story or a prayer, and then may sit in silence in the firelight, each one thinking his own thoughts. Or a group of children on a nature-wonder hike may play "the silent game,"[14] which gives any child the privilege of raising his hand at any moment on the trail through the woods if he wants the group to stand still and listen to "the stir of God in ocean and in wood."

In the use of silence, care should be taken that the periods of silence are not sustained longer than the span of the worshipers' attention. This can be safeguarded by introducing sufficient thought-enrichment, either visual or auditory. Auditory stimulation of the imagination is provided by music, the brief comments of a leader, or an occasional oral prayer. At times a picture which expresses the theme of the service may stand on the altar or hang before the group.

In all of these ways silence may make it possible for each worshiper to make his own approach to God.

In the stress and strain and hurry of modern life such periods of quiet relaxation are especially necessary. Periods of silence need to be carefully planned and directed if they are to prove stimulating.[15] The condi-

---

[14] See *Child and Universe*, by Bertha Stevens, p. 124. The John Day Company.

[15] See Fiske, *The Recovery of Worship*, Chap. XI, "The Religious Use of Silence."

Harris, *Christian Public Worship*, "A Service of Meditation" and "A Service of Silence."

Shaver and Stock, *Training Young People in Worship*, pp. 113-115.

tions created for worship should make silence seem the natural and desirable thing. We may devote an entire worship service to silent meditation. There are different methods of conducting such a service. It may take the form of a musical service, where worshipers silently take their seats and silently worship while one musical selection after another is played. Or some suggestions of a theme may be made, by handing each worshiper, as he enters, a brief quotation or a prayer for his thinking, as he listens to the music. One group of young people planned such a service for a spring vespers. Each worshiper received a mimeographed sheet containing Rauschenbusch's beautiful prayer of thanksgiving for the "universe our home," and the titles and composers of the musical selections, which were all interpretations of nature.

At other times the period of meditation may be introduced by a brief devotional talk to quicken the aspirations of the group and to suggest a specific trend for their thoughts to follow. After this there may be absolute silence or the playing of soft music, or alternate periods of silence and music. Such a service of meditation may conclude with a prayer by the leader or a unison prayer by the group.

Placing Prayer in the Worship Service. It may be well to remind ourselves of what was said in Chapter V about the arrangement of worship materials. The prayer in any service will be more challenging and be participated in more heartily if it is placed at that point where the group is emotionally ready for it. When new ideals have been glimpsed and aspirations have been kindled, then is the group ready to express its desires in the form of prayer.

Focusing Attention Upon the Prayer. Some suggestions for doing this have already been made in the section on the characteristics of prayer. It is often possible for a leader to arrest the attention of the group by a brief anecdote or some Scripture selection or some imaginative comment. In a service on "Heroes of Laughter," the leader introduces the prayer period by quoting Carlyle's statement, "Wondrous is the strength of cheerfulness." Then follows a brief quotation from one of Captain Scott's last letters, in which he speaks of the good cheer of his men as they are "pegging out in a very comfortless spot." After this introduction, the group is quite ready to pray for "the royalty of inward happiness and the serenity which comes from living close to thee."[16]

The Litany as One Form of Prayer. It is becoming increasingly common for nonliturgical churches to make use of the litany as one form of prayer. The litany has this advantage, that it deals with rather specific thanksgivings or requests and therefore lends itself to vivid word pictures which even the youngest can appreciate, and that its petitions or thanksgivings are divided into short sentences, each representing one thought, so that attention is easily held. Following is a section from such a litany, which is called:

AN EXPRESSION OF JOY

Leader: Let us praise God in gladness and humility for all great and simple joys.

Response: We thank Thee, O God. (To be repeated after each versicle.)

Leader: For the gift of wonder and the joy of discovery: for

---

[16] From *Prayers for Intermediate Worship*, Godfrey S. Pain, p. 38. Methodist Sunday School Department, London, England.

the everlasting freshness of experience: for the newness of life each day as we grow older,

Leader: For the fireside and the intimate talks of friendship: for the little traditions and customs of the home: for meals eaten together in fellowship: and for all the sanctities of family life.

Leader: For games and holidays in the open air: for bright eyes and lovely bodies: for books and pictures and all our small possessions,

Leader: For all pure comedy and laughter: for the gift of humor and gayety of heart,

Leader: For the image of Christ in ordinary people, their forbearance and their generosity, their good temper in crowds, their courage and their kindness,

Leader: For the glory of God shining in commonplace lives; for husband and wife scheming to please one another; for the sacrifices of both for their children,

Leader: For all holy and humble men of heart, in whom the loveliness of Jesus has been made manifest to the world.

These are merely suggestions of a few ways in which the principle of variety may be utilized in introducing prayer into the worship service. It is well for any leader not to fall into the habit of using any one method to the exclusion of others, and to remember that method is only a means by which prayer is kept meaningful and vital.

ADDITIONAL READING SOURCES

Brown, William Adams, *The Life of Prayer in a World of Science*. Charles Scribner's Sons.

Children's Prayers, Recorded by Their Mother. Pilgrim Press.

Fosdick, Harry Emerson, *The Meaning of Prayer*. Association Press.

Herman, E., *Creative Prayer*. James Clarke and Co., London.

Mather, Kirtley F., *Science in Search of God,* Chap. V. Henry Holt and Company.

Mumford, E. E. Read, *How We Can Help Children to Pray*. Longmans, Green & Co.

Page, Kirby, *Living Creatively*. Farrar & Rinehart.

Pain, Godfrey S., *Prayers for Junior Worship*. A. J. G. Seaton, London.

GUIDING THE EXPERIENCE OF WORSHIP

Stolz, Karl, *The Psychology of Prayer*. The Abingdon Press.

Streeter, Burnett Hillman, *Reality*, Chap. IX. The Macmillan Company.

Thayer, Mary Dixon, *The Child on His Knees*. The Macmillan Company. (Prayers of a Catholic child. While written in rhyme a few of them are excellent illustrations of the use of vivid word pictures in prayers.)

Collections of Prayers:

Allemann, Herbert C., *Prayers for Boys*. Henry Altemus Company.

Barstow, R. W., *Getting Acquainted With God*. The Macmillan Company.

Bartlett, Robert Merrill, *A Boy's Book of Prayers*. The Pilgrim Press.

Bragdon, Helen D., and Mattoon, Laura I. (Editors), *Services for the Open*. Century Company.

Children's Prayers, Recorded by Their Mother. The Pilgrim Press.

Hartshorne, Hugh, *Manual for Training in Worship*. Charles Scribner's Sons.

Hoyland, J. S., *A Book of Prayers,* written for use in an Indian College. The Challenge, Ltd., London.

Hoyland, J. S., *The Sacrament of Common Life*. W. Heffer & Sons, Ltd., Cambridge.

McComb, Samuel, *A Book of Modern Prayers*. Longmans, Green & Co.

Noyes, Morgan Phelps, *Prayers for Services*. Charles Scribner's Sons.

Orchard, W. E., *The Temple*. E. P. Dutton & Co.

Oxford University Press, *The Kingdom, the Power, and the Glory*.

Pain, Godfrey S., *Prayers for the Junior Church School*. A. J. G. Seaton, London.

Pain, Godfrey S., *Prayers for Intermediates*. A. J. G. Seaton, London.

Rauschenbusch, Walter, *Prayers of the Social Awakening*. The Pilgrim Press.

Scovil, Elizabeth, *Prayers for Girls*. Henry Altemus Company.

Student Christian Movement, *Learning to Pray*. A Book of School Prayers.

The Book of Common Prayer.

CHAPTER X

PREPARATION FOR WORSHIP

Lack of intense preparation of the soul accounts for the emptiness and feverishness of much that is regarded as religious, or at least as social, service. To expect the fruit of the Spirit without spiritual preparation for the same is to expect the impossible; it is to substitute mechanism for spirit. Religious faith cannot doubt that God is equally near to the souls of all men, to the grossest and dullest as well as to the most sensitive and obedient. Yet, though God be there, the miracle cannot happen to the unprepared soul. . . . The process of fruition comes only after a process of fertilization.—Edgar S. Brightman.

(In *Religious Values*. Used by permission of The Abingdon Press.)

It is a psychological principle which we all recognize as profoundly true that we get the most out of any life experience when we are "ready" for it. The child learns best that lesson which comes to him at the moment when his mind-set is receptive. It follows, then, that the worshiper who is intellectually and emotionally "ready" for worship, will participate in it more heartily and will derive greater enrichment from it than if he were totally unprepared.

Sometimes life itself brings this readiness. We come to worship with a conscious sense of need or desire. On the other hand, boys and girls and young people of early and middle adolescence often come to worship from a mixture of motives. They come, because it is a habit, because their friends come, because their parents want them to. In order that they may get the most out of the worship service, they need to be prepared in the sense that these motives are replaced by a real interest that is related to their life needs.

In departments where the entire program is very thoroughly integrated, the class sessions themselves may be a partial preparation for worship. In church schools where each grade has its own worship service, worship grows right out of the morning experience, and this involves a real preparation for worship. This is equally true of graded week-day schools. But even in graded situations, like these, there is a certain type of worship preparation which demands a special period for its accomplishment, such as the interpretation of material which is to be used in worship. And in schools where the departments are made up of three grades, each following slightly different lines of activity, a special period of preparation is essential in order that the group may be bound together by common purpose before they worship. In some church schools the entire department meets together for this period of preparation. In others each grade has a separate preparatory period, before they come together for a general department worship service.

THE NEED OF PREPARATION FOR WORSHIP

Let us see what such a period of preparation will be used for and try to discover why there is a need for such preparation.

The Need to Clarify Ideas. Since we worship best when our thinking is not confused, there is need that teachers and superintendents discover what ideas pupils have and then try to help them clarify their thinking. Through questions and answers in periods of preparation, the ideas of the group may be discovered.

Adequate Religious Concepts. We have seen in

Chapter III how early in life our concepts of God and of religious living are formed, and we have also seen how persistently some of these early formed concepts remain with us in later years. One important phase of preparation for worship consists of helping persons to acquire adequate concepts of God as a basis for a satisfying worship experience.

This sort of preparation can never be done adequately in just certain periods set aside and labeled as "preparation for worship." Rather, the entire program of religious education must be used to serve this end. Pictures, textbooks, the teaching of church-school teachers, the pastor's sermons, hymns, prayers—all of these may help to establish concepts of God which are beneficial. However, there are times when a department or a grade may profitably discuss together the problems arising from their ideas of God.

The Need of Creating Right Attitudes in the Worshiper. There are certain attitudes toward God which need to be cultivated in order that the worship experience may be more fruitful. The real importance of an individual's concepts of God lies in the influence which these concepts have upon his *attitude toward God*. Our attitude toward God is conditioned largely by what we think is God's attitude toward us. The way God *feels* and *thinks* and *acts* is far more important as a basis for worship than the way God *looks*. As our ideas about these things are clarified, we respond in worship with certain attitudes of our own.

If the worshiper comes to the worship service with certain attitudes, he will participate to better advantage. One of these attitudes is that of *anticipation*. We all know the part that interest plays in the individual's

227

ability to throw himself into any situation. In a period of preparation where pictures are associated with the Scripture to be memorized, where interesting stories are told about hymns and their composers, where the pupils are led through a stimulating music appreciation lesson, interest in the materials of worship is stimulated and the group looks forward to the worship service with anticipation.

There is need, also, for stimulating attitudes of security and trust. One of the first effects of worship is a relaxation of spirit, a loosening of tension, a feeling of quietness and of readiness for what worship has to offer us. This relaxation of spirit is brought about in part by the environment of worship and in part by the opening part of the service itself, with its quiet music and the Call to Worship.

But often in the short periods assigned to worship in children's and young people's groups, the service of worship alone is not sufficient for this type of preparation. Children and adolescents come to church school with such varying moods. They come from different home situations, not all of them conducive to the spirit of worship. Sometimes they come troubled by personal problems which intrude into consciousness and prevent the worshiper from entering into the worship experience.[1] This is true also of children in week-day schools of religion who come to the week-day class direct from the problems of the schoolroom and playground.

Experience as a Basis for Worship. Not only by adequate religious concepts and helpful attitudes is a satisfying worship experience made possible. We have seen repeatedly in the pages of this book how worship

[1] See Chap. II.

may flower out of the experiences of life. Since this is so, the best type of preparation for worship is a program of religious education which offers young and old a series of enriching religious experiences.

Doctor Hartshorne and Miss Lotz tell of the church-school group which entered into the experience of making a moving-picture reel depicting the "Growth of the Idea of God in the Old Testament."[2] This involved reading, research, discussion, writing of a scenario, posing the scenes, photographing them, developing the films, showing them to the group for evaluation and improvement, and finally lending the reel to other church schools so that their research on the subject might be shared by others. And then, one day, when this group of junior-high boys and girls had met to discuss whether it had been worth while to make the pictures, among other values worship was mentioned.

Edgar: I think the movies are very valuable for worship. It helped us to worship. When we went into the church and we had a hymn and read a parable, it helped us.
Several: Yes, very much. It helped me to worship.
David: It might be good to have a worship service before each time.[3]

If worship is to be really vital, it must arise as often as possible out of activities upon which we are all engaged. If each class in a department has certain specific class activities, then there should be certain enterprises in which all the classes unite. In the department period of preparation we discuss our common enterprise; we plan together for its fulfillment and in the light of the need of God which our task reveals, we

---

[2] See *Case Studies of Present-Day Religious Teaching*, pp. 194-203.
[3] *Case Studies of Present-Day Religious Teaching*, p. 201. Institute of Social and Religious Research, New York.

worship together. As we share tasks we are bound by a fellowship which makes it easier for us to worship together. It is possible too for a department in which each class is pursuing its own special interest to talk together in a departmental period about the individual class projects and to share the ideas they are getting from their class study. Each group from its special line of thought may contribute to the general group discussion. In this way each group within a larger group may share the best of its thought-life with all the others.

The Need for Appreciation of the Materials of Worship. It is only necessary to repeat here the truth that we enter more sincerely and heartily into worship if we understand the meaning of all hymns, Scripture, or responses, and if we have an appreciation of the music or any art forms used in the worship service.[4]

The Need for Memorizing Some of the Materials of Worship. The period of preparation should include far more than mere memory work. To memorize materials is only a small part of the preparation needed to make worship meaningful. But it is an important part, especially for children who are too young to do much reading or who are still at the age when the handling of papers and books detracts attention from the act of worshiping.

The content of the worship memory curriculum will vary with different age groups. Children through the primary department will memorize almost all worship materials, though the older primary groups may occasionally read from the board, or from printed copies.

In all age groups calls to worship and responses of various kinds are best memorized. Unison 'repetition

---

[4] See Chap. II.

of Scripture or poetry is often more meaningful in worship if memorized by the group, and when memorized it becomes the permanent possession of the individual which he may use in his hours of private worship.

There is a pleasure which comes from singing hymns without the aid of a hymnal. Children and young people need to be introduced to the joy of singing in this unhampered way. However, from the time when boys and girls enter the junior department and on through adolescence, it is scarcely possible to memorize all of the materials of worship which will be needed to meet the needs of the expanding religious life. We often hear it said that juniors require only a dozen hymns in a year for their worship experience. To confine juniors to only one dozen hymns for the expression of all the complex interests, desires, and conduct situations of boy and girl life to-day is a very limiting experience. If they are to enter into all the possibilities open to them of lives lived in companionship with God, we must offer them a richer variety of materials than they can possibly memorize even in quite long periods of preparation.

The Need of Preparation for Pupil Leadership. During the adolescent years we recognize the necessity of enlisting the initiative and creative ability of the young people themselves in planning the class and department program. This will include participation in the plans for worship. Adolescents need training and preparation for this type of leadership.

Since worship is so vast and far-reaching an experience, the young people ought to launch upon an investigation and study the whole subject as a basis of understanding for their leadership of worship. The worship committee should make a more minute study of the technique of worship, though if leadership of worship is to be passed around, the whole group needs the same training.[5]

In addition to this general study of what worship is and the principles underlying it, those responsible for planning and leading each service will need individual attention and help. There is no substitute for this personal weekly meeting of the adult adviser with the worship leaders when the service of worship is planned and all its details of leadership perfected. It is only in this way that real progress in worship is made possible.

"The thoughts of youth are long, long thoughts," and young people, even those of the intermediate age, are capable of doing some splendid leadership. But there is needed constantly the sympathetic advice of the adult leader who sees to it by his tactful but persevering supervision that the worship experience of the whole adolescent group does not sag because of the failure of some members to do their part or to do it well.

There should be opportunity in the adolescent group for frequent discussions about their worship services to discover whether they are meeting group needs and interests. This discussion should be constructive, not negative criticism, with suggestions for improvement stressed.

When the adolescent groups make their own investigation to discover their own needs of worship, the development of the worship life of the group becomes their own enterprise.

Shall children under the adolescent age plan and conduct worship services? There is probably no hard-and-

---

[5] For an excellent guide to a worship activity of this type, consult *Youth and Worship*, by E. L. Shaver. International Council of Religious Education.

fast answer to this question. It depends largely upon the character of the group, the method employed in the department (whether formal or informal), and the method by which such planning is done. Shall we have in children's groups pupil participation in planning and leading worship? It depends upon what they participate in. Are they, by so doing, participating in a worship experience or merely in a display of personal leadership powers? There is no doubt that boys and girls are capable of planning *programs*. They do this, even in third grades, for school assemblies in our more progressive schools.

But children cannot be expected to plan and lead *worship* if they are not given frequent opportunities for planning and leading *other* types of activities in the school program. Do they help to plan and lead the recreation of the class or department? How much opportunity is given for pupil initiative and leadership in class periods? Does the entire discipline of the department rest upon a basis of pupil co-operation and leadership, or is it purely of the autocratic type, enforced by adults? Unless the principle of the right of the child to a creative life in the school is observed throughout the entire school program, it is futile to talk in terms of real pupil creativity in the field of worship.

In certain departments where the whole educational process is of the child-centered type and where pupil activity is the keynote, one group of children might with their teacher plan a very beautiful worship service on some theme close to child life, for some Sunday morning. The teacher might explain in the simplest terms what our worship is for, and the children might suggest hymns, prayer, and other materials which they have learned to love. The planning would be group planning and the leadership with the teacher at the helm to sustain the feeling of worship.[6]

PREPARATION FOR PRIVATE WORSHIP

One of the objectives of the total worship program of the church is to make it possible for individuals to enjoy a more and more vital experience of worship in their private living. The individual should not be dependent upon public worship only to commune with God. There are moments when he very much needs to be alone with God. There are pressing, personal problems which he needs to think through with God's help. There are personal adjustments to make to circumstances in his own life situation, or to people, which can be made only in solitude.

The Need for Private Worship. Such hours of private worship are especially necessary in our own day, when our complex civilization keeps relentlessly pushing us into high-pressure activity. One of the definite goals of our worship program ought to be to reveal to people the need for these moments of private worship. We may begin with the boys and girls and help them gradually to build up the habit of private devotions. We may in our conferences with parents and in parents' meetings help the parents to learn how to make a place for quiet meditation in their own lives and how to make such periods for quiet relaxation attractive to children.

The Need for a Technique of Private Worship. One reason why few people have habits of regular private worship is that when they *are* alone, they do not know

[6] *As Children Worship*, by Jeannette E. Perkins. The Pilgrim Press.

what to do with their solitude. People sometimes refrain from private devotions because they feel the need of devotional material to stimulate their thought and are unfamiliar with the sources of such material.

In order, then, to provide a well-rounded-out worship experience for each person, the program of worship training in the church should include definite suggestions as to *how* the individual can most effectively conduct his private worship. These suggestions will have to be graded to the ages of the different groups of worshipers. A technique of private worship needs to be worked out for children and adolescents,[7] helpful as Doctor Wieman's book on *Methods of Private Religious Living* is for adults.[8] A step in this direction is the establishing of the "Children's Prayer Corner" in many Protestant Episcopal churches. This is a corner set aside for the children, where there are worship pictures on the wall—pictures that will appeal to childhood—a few prayers, attractively illuminated, and books of poems and stories. There is a prayer bench and a sign which says:

> Be very quiet, please.
> Touch and look at anything you like.
> Kneel for one prayer before you go.

Such a stimulating reminder of God in the midst of the activities of life might be introduced into any community house or educational plant of the church. A table over which hangs a devotional picture and on which are lying a few well-chosen devotional books may

[7] For suggestions for young people, see article, "Helping Youth in Personal Devotions," by Henry N. Wieman, in the *International Journal of Religious Education*, May, 1929.

[8] See pamphlet, "Methods of Personal Devotions," Board of Education of Methodist Episcopal Church, 740 Rush Street, Chicago. Ill.

arrest the attention of those who are gathering for meetings or waiting for friends.

The worship committee of a young people's department might utilize such a worship corner to suggest to the young people helpful materials for use in their personal devotions. Some young people's groups have, from time to time, supplied their members with mimeographed sheets containing devotional poetry or prose and prayers.

Following is an example of the type of help which one minister gave the members of his adult congregation for their use every day. These worship suggestions were printed on an attractive card which could be hung over a desk or lie on a table. The card contained thoughts for the early morning, for the middle of the day, and for the evening hours.

CHRISTIAN WATCHWORDS
FOR EVERYDAY LIVING

At Night

The day, with the work God gave me to do, is done and now he has given me the night, quiet and beautiful for rest. I will therefore trust myself, body and spirit, into his loving, tender care through the mystery of sleep. I am God's child. As flood tides from the ocean fill each bay or inlet, so power and love and peace can fill my life to overflowing as I rest quietly in him. Because I am God's child I will rest in him quietly, serenely, patiently, bravely, lovingly, with confidence and perfect self-control.

In the Morning

All this day I am going to be a child of God. His love is round about me. Underneath are the everlasting arms. I am going to be honest and true in all events of life and I believe that to those who love God all things work together for good. I am going to rise above all worry, fretting, fear and hatred, and live in an atmosphere of spiritual serenity. My life is not apart from the life of God, and that which is divine within me can never fail or be defeated. Behind all that comes God's love and wisdom will be present to strengthen and sustain.[9]

The daily Bible readings incorporated in some lesson courses might be made much more helpful for devotional use if they were selected with reference to the pupil's actual interests and problems of living, if they were truly *devotional* selections, and if interesting suggestions for their use were given.

Boys and girls can make their own books of private devotions, by collecting poems, Psalms, prayers, and hymns which they especially like and by illustrating these with appropriate pictures.

The Period of Preparation for Worship

When shall the period of preparation occur? There are several choices, the exact time depending upon the equipment and procedure of individual schools. Let us bear in mind as we talk about *"a period of preparation for worship"* that the entire program of religious education ought to be a preparation for worship. Let us remember that this preparation may be going on in every class period, through every enterprise participated in, in all of the educative experiences offered the members of a church. But we are thinking now of some period when a class, meeting separately, or the different classes comprising a department, meet for the purpose of sharing ideas, plans, or appreciation experiences, so that they may be more united in the act of worship.

How shall we distinguish between "preparation for worship" and worship itself? Often such a distinction

---

[9] Dr. Albert W. Palmer. Used by permission.

is impossible. When, on a spring Sunday, we are thrilling to the joy of life, as we read and then memorize:

"For lo, the winter is past. The rain is over and gone. The flowers appear on the earth. The time of the singing of birds is come,"

we suddenly feel very conscious of God's presence. We have called this a period of preparation for worship; but suddenly we find that we *are* worshiping. Often in informal periods of appreciation, such spontaneous moments of worship are felt. The leader should be sensitive to this and allow the group all the expression of this worship feeling which it craves. We may pause in the midst of our memorizing to offer a prayer of thanksgiving or to sing "This Is My Father's World."

One morning a visitor, interested in the worship program of the church school, arrived at a second-grade primary room, to find the children busily constructing a model of the village of Nazareth. This was in a church school organized by the grade plan, each grade having a very flexible program. The teacher, as she greeted the visitor, said: "Oh, I am so sorry. I know you want to see the worship service and we're not going to worship this morning. We're going to spend all our time on our village and on the stories of Jesus." *"We are not going to worship this morning."* How did she know? How could she tell? As a matter of fact, those boys and girls were very near to worship more than once during the morning.

The Sunday-Morning Period. A period of from twenty to thirty minutes may be set aside on Sunday morning in each department as a period of preparation for worship. This implies an entire morning period of at least one and one-half hours. Many schools are experimenting with church programs which occupy the entire Sunday-morning period.

The Week-Day Period. Where groups meet during the week, the week-day period may be used for the study and appreciation of worship materials and the discussion and carrying out of projects which are linked to worship. If this is the only period of preparation for worship, it has this disadvantage—that, so far as the cultivation of attitudes is concerned, there may not be a real carry-over from the middle of the week to the Sunday-morning session.

The Sunday-Evening Period. For adolescent groups which have evening meetings of their departments, in the form of young people's societies or forums, this Sunday-evening period occasionally may be devoted to preparation for worship. It need not be called by that name, but the materials introduced into the evening session might be planned by the program committee with the definite idea of their correlation with the morning worship services.

There might be a series of evening sessions devoted to a study of worship for young people.[10] There might be a series of meetings where the subject of prayer might be discussed, in the attempt to solve the problems which the group raises about prayer. The worship committee might then, on the basis of these evening discussions, plan the worship services for the Sunday mornings on some theme related to Prayer, a theme growing out of the discussion of the previous week. There might be a

[10] See "Christian Quest Series"—Youth at Worship. Also, *Everyday Adventures for Intermediates*, Unit J-3—"What Shall We Sing?" Unit K-1—"Problems of Prayer." The Methodist Book Concern, 740 Rush Street, Chicago, Illinois.

series on "Our Ideas of God," including "Ideas of God in Our Hymns," "Ideas of God in Our Prayers," "Ideas of God in the Bible," "Ideas of God Gained From Science," etc.

Occasionally the Sunday evenings may be given over to music appreciation under the leadership of a trained musician. One high-school department in a church school has one Sunday evening a month devoted to music appreciation, developed by the supervisor of music in the local high school.

METHODS USED IN PREPARATORY PERIODS

Since the objectives of a period of preparation for worship are to deepen appreciation of the worship materials, to prepare the worshipers for worship by arousing helpful attitudes, to assist in the memorization of certain materials, and to make possible for the group the greatest possible participation in the worship experience, the methods used will be those which will contribute to these ends.

The period of preparation is, above everything else, a friendly, informal, active period. It ought to be a thoroughly enjoyable period, so that *desire* for worship is aroused.

Conversation. Informal conversation provides for a hearty response and participation by the pupils. Conversation differs from the mere asking and answering of questions, in that pupils are not called on formally, but the leader tells a story, makes a comment, or asks a question; the pupils' thinking processes are started and they want to talk about it.

The Appreciation Method. The period of preparation may be devoted to appreciation of music, of pictures, of hymns, of Scripture, whatever will most enrich the worship service to follow. Appreciation means enjoyment. To understand the inner meaning of art, literature, or poetry is to thrill to their message for us.

The problem of the leader in an appreciation period is to help the group to understand meanings without too much critical analysis. The appreciation period is for the purpose of revealing the beauty or the significance that lies at the heart of a great experience and every moment of the period should yield enjoyment to the group.

The Story Method. The story method will be used over and over in periods of preparation for worship. Sometimes it will be the story of a musical composer or an artist. Or it may be the story of a specific picture. Often a well-chosen and well-told story will arouse a desirable attitude. Again, a story may focus the interest of the group on a certain part of the worship service. It may stimulate interest in the selection which is to be learned. Or a story may set the group to thinking about some challenging problem which will need the worship experience for its solution.

The Discussion Method. When as a basis for worship ideas are to be clarified or enterprises planned or the significance of certain problems realized, the period of preparation may take the form of discussion.

The Creative Method. The period of preparation affords an opportunity for a class or department to engage in some creative activity in the field of worship. Worship services can be planned, prayers, litanies or responsive services composed or worship materials can be searched for and pasted in Books of Worship which the pupils can make for use in their services.

Memorization. Memorization as a method of preparation for worship needs to be carefully used. The moment memory work becomes distasteful, in that moment it starts to inhibit the worship attitude. Memorization, as a basis for participation in worship, should be kept on the appreciation level. If unpleasant associations are built up around a hymn, a poem, or a passage of Scripture because the method of memorizing them has been uninteresting or positively distasteful, these unpleasant associations will make it impossible for the worshiper to enjoy them in worship.

ADDITIONAL READING SOURCES

Blashfield, Clara Beers, *Worship Training for Primary Children.* Chapter V, "Instrumental Music and Pictures." The Methodist Book Concern.

Clark, Glenn, *The Soul's Sincere Desire.* Atlantic Monthly Press.

Cross, Edward M., *The Use of Religion.* Church Publishing House, Spokane, Wash.

Crandall, Edna, *A Curriculum of Worship for the Junior Church School.* D. Appleton-Century Company.

Department of Epworth League, Methodist Episcopal Church, *Everyday Adventures for Intermediates.*

(a) The Worship Service   (d) Problems of Prayer
(b) The Poetry Trail   (e) Communion
(c) What Shall We Sing?

Hartman, G., and Shumaker, A., *Creative Expression.*

Hurll, Estelle, *How to Show Pictures to Children.* Houghton Mifflin Company.

International Council of Religious Education, *The Christian Quest Series.*

(a) Youth at Worship
(b) Youth and Story Telling

Klar and Dillaway, *The Appreciation of Pictures.* Brown-Robertson Company, New York.

Mearns, Hughes, *Creative Power.* Doubleday, Doran and

Company. *Creative Youth.* Doubleday, Doran and Company.

Myers, A. J. W., *Teaching Religion Creatively.*. Fleming H. Revell Company.

Powell, Marie Cole, "Worship Suggestions for Juniors," *International Journal of Religious Education,* issues March, 1932–September, 1933.

Powell, Marie Cole, *Junior Method in the Church School.* The Abingdon Press.
> Chap. XII, "Learning to Appreciate."
> Chap. XIII, "Building Character Through Creative Work."
> Chap. XIV, "Education Through Drill."
> Chap. XVII, "Teaching Through Pictures."

Shaver, Erwin L., *Youth and Worship.* International Council of Religious Education.

Smither, Ethel, *Teaching Primaries in the Church School.* The Methodist Book Concern.
> Chap. IX, "The Use of Poems, Songs and Music During the Class Sessions"; Chap. X, "Developing Group Purpose Through Conversations"; Chap. XI, "Using Pictures to Help Children Learn."

Wieman, Henry N., *Methods of Private Religious Living.* The Macmillan Company.

Wilkinson, Marguerite, *New Voices.* (Helpful in poetry appreciation.)

CHAPTER XI

THE LEADERSHIP OF WORSHIP

A little child has listened at my breast
  And, finding rhythms too dull to match her own,
Has taught me quicker, quainter ones, unguessed.
  So has she glimpsed my mind a monotone
And brought me piquant hues with which to twine
  My thoughts—gayer than I alone could know;
In fashions, then, I hardly claim for mine,
  More radiant, more rich, more wise I go.

But where her eyes have never searched me yet—
  Where my vexed spirit gropes unknown to her,
I need His vigilance—lest I forget,
  In all my cluttered living, in the whir
Of deafening trifles, in each day's long din—
  To have an altar there—when she looks in!

—CHARLOTTE HUNGERFORD PERRY.
("Caroline," in *Good Housekeeping*.)

THE preceding chapters of this book will have failed in their most important function if they have not renewed in us a consciousness of the seriousness of our task; if they have not led us to realize as never before the need of intensive preparation for the leadership of worship.

It is perfectly obvious that he who would plan and lead worship must have, first of all, a genuine experience of worship in his own life. We must "have an altar there," when children and young people look to us for leadership. To know every day in our own life experience that "never alone is the Christian who lives by faith and prayer" gives us the assurance to try to make this conviction real to others.

THE LEADERSHIP OF WORSHIP

One of the things which we soon come to realize is that the experience of leading others in worship is retroactive. We grow in our own personal religious life as we make our plans for a worship program for others.

As leaders in religious education, we are concerned that our worship program shall be constantly reaching higher and higher levels of attainment. If worship is, as many feel, the very heart of all religious experience, then we must devote untiring energy and the best critical thought of which we are capable to its continuous improvement.

The Responsibility for Improvement. Who is responsible for the improvement of the worship program of the church? Of course, the pastor is responsible for the worship of the adult Sunday congregations. He ought to be in a position to be very helpful to the church-school staff at this point, and some pastors who have made a special study of worship are. However, it is possible for a minister to be able to plan and conduct very effective worship services for the adults and yet to fail to understand the worship interests and needs of childhood and youth. As our theological seminaries begin to include more courses for ministers in the religious education of youth, we shall hope for real leadership from ministers in this field.

Usually in the church school the general superintendent and the department superintendent are those who bear the heaviest responsibility for developing and improving the worship program. In schools following the grade rather than the departmental plan, the grade teachers assume the leadership of worship along with the teaching function. All such leaders are vitally concerned with deepening their own understand-

245

ing of worship and improving their ability to plan and lead it.

We have already seen how teachers should share in the task of developing the worship program of a department. Teachers too are responsible for bringing to the richest possible fruition the worship experiences of their own classes. Often there are in the church, club or group leaders who have an opportunity to lead their groups into worship experiences. These leaders should consult with teachers of church-school classes and arrive at some co-operative plans for improving the worship curriculum of the church.

Worship committees of adult groups and of young people's departments and societies are also interested in and responsible for improving the worship services of their groups.

Education for Leadership. This placing of responsibility reveals the need for a far-reaching program of education in worship. In summer schools of religious education or in community or church training schools leaders may take courses in the theory and practice of worship. The worship program of any church will be greatly strengthened if teachers as well as those who are directly responsible for leading worship would enter such courses. Then there could be a far more intelligent piece of co-operative work done by teachers and superintendents.

The leader's preparation need not stop with attendance at classes. He will find it stimulating to his own religious growth as well as helpful in his planning of worship to read the new books which come off the press in the field of worship and those which express the best thought of our times on the nature of God, the psychology of prayer, and the relation of worship to thought and feeling and conduct. Any leader of worship ought to read as regularly as possible the articles on worship and the worship suggestions in his own denominational magazines and in those which are interdenominational. Some of these journals carry stimulating accounts of how other leaders are guiding the worship experiences of their groups.

In addition there is the necessity of being constantly on the lookout for new worship materials: a new story-book, a better hymnal than the one we are using, suggested worship programs in our religious educational magazines, an idea caught as we are reading a book some day—an idea which, modified and enriched, may be the basis of a worship service some Sunday. The wise superintendent will have a file or a scrapbook in which to record that elusive idea, that story or that piece of music, for future reference.

THE PROBLEM OF SUPERVISION

Supervision of Worship. Some churches are fortunate in having the services of a trained director of religious education who conceives of his task in terms of supervision, and who can become the "helping teacher" in matters of worship as well as in teaching procedure. Some churches have leaders of ability whom they send to summer schools of religious education or to community or denominational training schools, where they can specialize in the courses in worship and in supervision and so prepare themselves to render valuable service in their local churches. When such help is not available, there may be occasional visits of a denominational secretary who can observe the worship services and meet with the leader and teachers afterward for conference, offering suggestions for improvement.

Sharing the Task of Leadership

A leader need not carry alone the burden of preparation for worship nor the responsibility for its outcomes. The best leadership is that which is willing to share responsibility with others.

If worship is to meet the needs of any group, it will be most successful if all the teaching staff share with the leader in studying the group needs, in formulating the objectives for the worship program, in making suggestions for specific services, and in checking up and evaluating the outcomes. The leader who thus shares the planning of worship will begin to feel that he is sustained and upheld by a spirit of eagerness and enthusiasm on the part of his teaching staff which will be felt by the pupils as well. One superintendent of an intermediate department, who has always conceived of her task of leadership as a "sharing endeavor," meets with her teachers every Sunday morning at quarter past nine for a brief worship service before they meet their pupils for the morning's work. So much do these teachers feel that *all the work* of the department is *their* work that they are eager to gather fifteen minutes early to share a worship experience of their own as a source of inspiration for their leadership.

The superintendent of the school or of a department may enlist the co-operation of the pupils also in the preparation for worship. Pupils may share the responsibility for preparing the room, distributing hymnals, arranging flowers or pictures, or caring for the altar, if there is one. Pupils' committees may be assigned certain duties, such as welcoming and introducing strangers, ushering, or taking care of late-comers.

But let us not forget that the main object of the leader's preparation is that he may be physically, mentally and spiritually ready himself to worship, and then to lead the group in worship. He should utilize the organization of the church school to the best advantage to secure for himself freedom from engrossing detail just before he is to lead in worship. Duties should be distributed among secretaries and student and teacher committees, so that the leader may be able to complete his arrangements for worship, to establish friendly contacts with pupils and teachers, and to create an atmosphere in which the fullest possibilities of worship can be realized.

FOLLOWING UP THE WORSHIP SERVICES

Because worship has been so often thought of as an experience almost altogether separated from the rest of the religious educational program, there has been a tendency to set it off by itself with little preparation for it and still less follow-up to ascertain whether its aims have been realized. Doctor Hartshorne and Miss Lotz have rightly placed it as an integral part of the total program when, in listing a series of questions by which one may evaluate the learning-teaching experiences in the church school, among all the other questions we find this one: "Is experience interpreted in worship?"[1] However, since worship has its own special functions in the total program of religious education, we must have some effective methods of seeing that all the purposes of wor-

[1] See *Case Studies of Present-Day Religious Teaching,* p. 194. Yale University Press.

ship are fulfilled in individual and in group experience and of discovering whether these methods are achieving the results we are after.

Results to Be Sought Through Worship. The results which we seek through an all-round worship experience are those which are expressed in the aims of worship described in Chapter I.[2] These aims are far-reaching and are not to be thought of as existing in addition to or outside of the aims of the total curriculum of religious education. They are an integral part of the program and take their place along with the aims for Christian character building to be achieved through study, discussion and activity.

As we study the laws of habit, we see clearly that worship is only one part of the whole learning process and that if worship is to achieve its richest results in making lives more God-conscious and more God-like, other processes must come in to help. Of prayer, Mrs. Blashfield says, "The complete act is purposing, planning, executing and judging. Prayer is not really complete unless it goes into activity."[3] So, worship to be a complete act should arise out of pupil purposes and needs and continue through to complete expression in the attitude and conduct of the individual.

When a series of worship services is aimed to develop an appreciation of honesty as a Christian ideal and the child thrills to this ideal and really wants to be honest, it is folly to send him home to a situation where he may receive no help in being honest but possibly positive temptation to dishonesty. We are morally bound, as religious educators, to do something about the home

[2] See also the chart in the Appendix.
[3] See *Worship Training for Primary Children*, p. 165. The Methodist Book Concern.

situation. We cannot be content to emotionalize the child's attitudes through worship and expect him to be able to meet situations which are beyond his capacity for solution. We must follow up the worship experience by our program of home visitation and conference with the parents.

We say that we expect worship to stimulate high resolves which are to be carried out in life activity. But, we cannot be sure how long the emotional propulsion of a worship service will be effective in motivating right conduct. The more immediate the opportunity for living out the new resolve stimulated by worship, the greater the probability that worship will really help to build the character. The church is under the necessity of providing through its program opportunities for individual and corporate Christian activity in order that its members may actually experience the close relationship of worship and conduct.

Observing the Results of Worship. There are certain opportunities which teachers and superintendents have to observe whether the worship services are finding fruition in improved personal living, in a growing companionship with God, or in a greater capacity for social vision and action.

Attitudes and Conduct During the Worship Service. Some of these opportunities will come in the worship service itself. In the prayer and in the dedicatory hymns the worshiper voices his intention to be more helpful or more loyal or more grateful. By this word-repetition the new goal for conduct is fixed in consciousness.

But this alone will not build Christian character. The first place where we may expect improvement in conduct is in the worship service itself. What of the child who sings,

> "At school, at home we follow thee
> With all our heart and soul.
> Work hard, play fair, and try to be
> Like thee in self-control,"[4]

and then is a disturber in the worship service? He is a disturber because he needs help in building habits of self-control. The whole religious education program must come in here to assist the teachers in understanding the child and his background and to discover the methods which will help him achieve self-control.

We are assuming, of course, that everything possible has been done to make the worship experience what it should be to meet the needs of the child's group. Often a child is a disturber in worship because the worship program itself is at fault.

Improved Conduct in the Class Session and Group Meetings. There may be the pupil who sings,

> "O Master of the loving heart,
> The friend of all in need,
> We pray that we may be like thee
> In thought and word and deed"—[5]

and this same pupil may in the class session following worship show his unfriendly attitude to another member of the class in all three ways, "thought," "word," and "deed."

So the class session itself becomes a supreme opportunity for the teacher to help the pupil to live out the attitudes of friendliness, helpfulness, and co-operation

---

[4] By A. M. Pullen. Used by permission. No. 79 in *Junior Church School Hymnal*. Presbyterian Board of Christian Education.

[5] By Calvin W. Laufer, in *Junior Church School Hymnal*. Presbyterian Board of Christian Education. Used by permission of author.

which worship has stimulated. We need never hope, as superintendents and teachers, that Christian character will be made as a result of our teaching, *outside the church school,* unless we can see that it is made while the child is *in the church school.* We shall only succeed in fostering insincerity in the religious experience if we stimulate through worship ideals of noble living and then do not help our youth to begin at once to live out those ideals right where they are in church school or department.

Whenever teachers of religion meet with their groups in activities of play, work, exploration, or service, there are opportunities to follow up the worship services by noticing changes in attitudes or conduct, tendencies to interpret experiences through worship, or increasing desire or ability to Christianize human relationships. Pupils can also evaluate their own worship experiences.

Helpful Methods. In attempting to follow up worship there are different methods which a leader may use. *Informal conversation* in a friendly group atmosphere will reveal what pupils are thinking or feeling. A few moments at the beginning of class sessions for discussion of the worship service are often helpful. "What did you like best about the worship service this morning?" asks the teacher. Or, "Did our worship service make you think of anything we were discussing last week?" Or, "Wasn't it strange that our worship service helped to answer the question John asked a few Sundays ago?" By questions like this thought may be stimulated and responses to the value or interest of the worship services solicited. In such group discussions the leader can often discover questions which are puzzling individuals, ideas which need clarifying, interest or lack of interest in the worship service as well as suggestions for further worship experiences.

There are *tests* which can be used to ascertain ideas and attitudes. Although tests are not infallible in their accuracy, they often reveal concepts, ideas and attitudes which indicate to the leaders the direction in which needs lie.

Conferences with parents or others who know the pupil are invaluable in assisting the leader to understand the interests and needs of individuals. Many parents will respond with eagerness to the suggestion that through worship we are trying to help each pupil to live at his best and to assume a satisfying relationship to God. Some parents will be glad of definite help in enriching the worship life of the home. Through parent-teacher meetings both parents and teachers may see how fundamental to the experience of worship are the contacts which they make with the boys and girls and young people.

By *observation* when groups are playing or discussing among themselves or working upon enterprises, a wise leader may learn much about the failure or success of the worship program to function in the lives of pupils.

EVALUATING THE WORSHIP PROGRAM

Worship, like all other experiences, will only improve as we are able to evaluate it from time to time. We have seen how a competent supervisor may offer invaluable help at this point. Where no supervisor is available, the leader himself will have to attempt to view the worship services as objectively as possible and to evaluate them. He will be greatly aided if he will avail himself of the suggestions from the teachers in the department. If the planning of the worship program is a co-operative enterprise shared by superintendent and teachers, then all together may use an observation sheet of some kind, and after each one has checked it, this may be used as a basis for discussion in staff meetings.[6]

The chief value of any observation sheet is that it shall tell its story objectively and stimulate us to better endeavor. The bibliography at the end of this book suggests several such guides which are available and helpful.

We have already seen that even young children can evaluate their own worship experiences, and no evaluation of worship is worthy the name that does not include the appraisal of the members of the worshiping group as well as that of the leaders. When any group shares in setting up the objectives for worship and in planning the services, they will inevitably respond to the idea of setting up standards for its improvement.

Records as a Means of Evaluation. Complete records should be kept of the objectives of worship for each year, written descriptions of any problems or situations which the worship services were planned to meet and copies of each worship service, including all the materials used (as stories, hymns, music, prayers, responses). The records should include notations of questions asked, remarks made or conduct responses by individuals or groups which seem to reveal needs that can be met through worship. Class teachers can supply for these records reactions of the pupils to the worship services, as they are discussed informally in class.

[6] See the *International Standards in Religious Education,* sections on Worship.

The leader will covet for these records the impartial and helpful criticisms of some competent observer, who participates sympathetically in the worship services and helps the leader to evaluate these experiences. In all of these ways can the leader of worship use the past experiences of worship in the group as stepping-stones to higher levels of worship.

CONDUCTING THE SERVICE OF WORSHIP

Every leader ought to grow in his ability to conduct a service of worship smoothly, to hold the attention of the group, or, if working with adolescents, to develop their latent capacities for leadership.

The Leader's Manner. The leader may suggest worship by his very attitude, and he may also suggest that the worship service is something which he anticipates with happiness, and so he passes on his sense of pleasure to the group. He may also suggest by his very manner that he expects quiet and participation.

He will study the best tone of voice to use, not artificially, but sincerely, knowing that his voice must be loud enough to be heard by the individual seated in the very last seat, but that his tone should suggest quiet, reverence, repose.

The wise leader will learn the art of waiting. Pauses are sometimes the most successful of educational methods. No story until everyone is sitting quiet and relaxed. No opening prayer or call to worship until every bit of whispered conversation is silenced.

No matter what the environment of worship, it is important that the leader himself be worshiping at every moment of the service. He cannot be worshiping if he is hunting for a misplaced hymnal, fumbling his notes, giving belated instructions to the workers, or indulging in low-toned conversation with the assistant leader. Yet, who has not seen these very evidences of lack of preparation even in ministers who should have known better?

Attention to Details. The importance of attention to details in the planning and conduct of worship cannot be overemphasized. For beauty of environment and well-chosen worship materials may fail to create a worshipful service if the leader is careless about the technique of worship. Many a worship service has been seriously impaired by lack of attention to details.

A chapel with an altar and a pulpit and lectern requires a certain type of usage. In such an environment the leader must understand where to stand for each part of the service. A senior high-school group whose worship services were to be held in a Gothic chapel, spent some time studying the Gothic setting of their worship services, so that they might observe the correct usage when they were the leaders of worship.

Ministers who have paid little attention to the conduct of worship sometimes build Gothic churches which demand a certain type of procedure, with which they are unfamiliar. The minister who is ignorant of or indifferent to this correct procedure in such an ecclesiastical environment strikes a jarring note which is incongruous.

There are other details which may make or mar the perfection of a worship service. Some of them seem almost too trivial to mention, yet the frequency with which they are neglected or overlooked seems to indicate that their importance is underestimated. There is a technique with regard to the making of announcements.

There is really no place for them in a worship service. The increasingly common usage of a church paper carrying all announcements obviates this difficulty as far as the morning worship of the church congregation is concerned. In church schools bulletin boards can be used or oral announcements made to the separate classes or in some departmental period other than the worship period.

Interruptions of all kinds should be avoided. To secure freedom from interruptions, the leader of worship will often have to be very firm in his attitude. There should be in every department of the church school one or two who are stationed at the entrances to safeguard the uninterrupted quiet of the worship period. In departments where pupil ushers are used there should be at least one tactful adult of mature experience to act as adviser when situations become too involved for pupil control.

The removal of outside wraps, whenever possible, makes it much easier for boys and girls to worship. Indeed, many an adult congregation would find itself better able to co-operate actively in the act of worship if their bodies were perfectly comfortable, as they often cannot be under the pressure of too much clothing. We would not attempt to undertake other types of creative work with our hats and coats on. Yet we try to concentrate our attention upon the most vital of all creative acts—worship—with these distracting encumbrances annoying us.

Many a worship service is robbed of its greatest influence upon the worshipers because of lack of fresh air or failure to have the right temperature. Children are often restless or unresponsive, and adults become drowsy, just because of these defects in the physical environment. It is a great pity that a well-planned worship service should fail to meet the worship needs of a group, when the opening of a window might not only minister to the needs of the body, but might also mean the opening of the windows of the soul, which is even more important.

Let us think, then, of our task as leaders of worship in terms of helping every individual to achieve the most satisfying relationship to God which is possible for him. Let us, so far as we are able, provide for our boys and girls and young people an environment of worshipful beauty which will kindle their aspirations and make them conscious of God's presence. Let us guide them in their thoughts about God that they may have such adequate concepts of him and of the religious life that God will be to them a living reality and that their relationship to him will express itself in genuine growth in Christian character. Let us spare no effort in perfecting ourselves in the art of worship, that we may be able to provide in our churches a satisfying and enriching worship experience for children, youth, and adults. Let us seek to minister to the religious needs of our groups, not through public worship alone, but by helping individuals to find God in their hours of solitary worship and to carry with them an awareness of his presence through all the activities of their lives. And, last of all, let us dedicate ourselves to the leadership of worship as those responding to a divine calling, and may our very act of dedication mean the acceptance by each one of us of the challenge to enter, in our own personal living, upon that greatest of all adventures—a growing companionship with the living God.

GUIDING THE EXPERIENCE OF WORSHIP

ADDITIONAL READING SOURCES

Athearn, Laura Armstrong, *Christian Worship for American Youth,* Chap. XI, "Creating an Atmosphere of Worship." D. Appleton-Century Company.

Baker, Edna Dean, *Worship of the Little Child.* Cokesbury Press.

Blashfield, Clara Beers, *Worship Training for Primary Children,* Chap. II, "Leaders of Worship." The Abingdon Press.

Chave, Ernest J., *Supervision of Religious Education,* Chap. VIII. University of Chicago Press.

Elbin, Paul N., *The Improvement of College Worship.* Bureau of Publications, Columbia University.

Hartshorne, Hugh, and Lotz, Elsa, *Case Studies of Present-Day Religious Teaching.* Yale University Press.

Jones, Mary Alice, *Training Juniors in Worship.* Cokesbury Press.

Katz, Daniel, Allport, F. H., and Jenness, M. B., *Students' Attitudes.* The Craftsman Press, Syracuse, N. Y.

Perkins, Ruth, *Planning Services of Worship.* Woman's Press.

Shaver, E. L., and Stock, H. T., *Training Young People in Worship,* Chap. IX, "Preparing For and Leading Worship." The Pilgrim Press.

Tests and Evaluation Sheets:

Board of Christian Education, *How to Study Individual Growth.*

Chave, Ernest J., University of Chicago. Worship Evaluation Tests.

International Council of Religious Education—Standards.

McLean, Angus H., *Ideas of God in Protestant Religious Education.* Bureau of Publications, Columbia University.

Thurstone, L. L., *Scales for the Measurement of Social Attitudes.* University of Chicago Press.

APPENDIX A

THE NATURE OF WORSHIP

A. Von Ogden Vogt

1. Vision or Ecstasy.
2. Humility or Repentance.
3. Recollection.
4. Vitality or Salvation.
5. Illumination or Clarification.
6. Enlistment or Dedication.
7. Peace.

B. Edgar S. Brightman

There are four stages of worship:
1. Reverent contemplation.
2. Revelation.
3. Communion.
4. Fruition.

C. Rollo Schloerb

Worship is:
An outreaching of the self toward God.
Thinking about the things which concern God and our-selves.
Some attitude toward these things definitely taken.

D. Hugh Hartshorne

1. Review, either deliberate or forced, of what has taken place.
2. Attention to what might have taken place.
3. Re-evaluation of the past, by contrast with the ideal.
4. Regret that what might have been was not. Sometimes accompanied by feeling of strain and estrangement.
5. Identification with the ideal—Consequent feeling of forgiveness and worth.
6. Recovery or Achievement of Peace—Sense of fellowship with God, Unity with Mankind.

E. HENRY N. WIEMAN

> In worship man deliberately undertakes to make the best possible adjustment to the matter of greatest concern—God.

> Private Worship is doing two things:
> 1. Finding out what is wrong with oneself.
> 2. Establishing that personal attitude through which one can receive from sources outside himself those influences which will correct wrong in him.

> What is involved in the act of Private Worship?
> 1. Relaxation and awareness of that upon which we are dependent.
> 2. Call to mind the possibilities for good which are inherent in the process called God.
> 3. Face the chief problem with which we are struggling.
> 4. Self-analysis to find what change must be made in mental attitudes and personal habits. Worship enables us to discover what personal readjustment is necessary in ourselves. In worship we are finding a way to join ourselves with God in his work of integration.
> 5. Formulate in words as clearly as possible the readjustment of personality and behavior that is required.

F. HARRISON ELLIOT

> Creative worship consists of the following steps:
> 1. A situation or problem of real concern.
> 2. An earnest desire to discover a course of action or an attitude which will be true to the highest values one recognizes—these values for most Christians being personified in God, the will of God, and Jesus' way of life.
> 3. A willingness and a desire not only to find the meaning of this scale of values in this situation, but to re-examine this scale of values itself.
> 4. A willingness to accept and act on that which is discovered and which comes to be one's conviction as the right or best or truest course of action.
> 5. A consciousness of personal friendship with the personal embodiment of their ideals, the God in whom they believe.

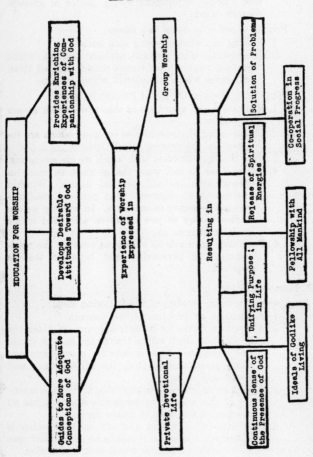

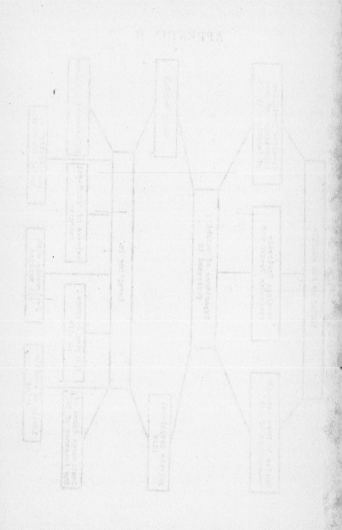

DATE DUE